A Wesley Reader

Writings of John and Charles Wesley

A WESLEY READER

WRITINGS OF JOHN AND CHARLES WESLEY

selected and edited
by Ted A. Campbell

Tuckapaw Media
Dallas, Texas
2008

A WESLEY READER:
WRITINGS OF JOHN AND CHARLES WESLEY

Selected and Edited by Ted A. Campbell
Special materials copyright © 2008, Ted A. Campbell
All rights reserved worldwide

ISBN: 0-9820698-0-4
EAN-13:   978-0-9820698-0-6

Date of version: 6 December 2008

Tuckapaw Media
Dallas, Texas
http://tuckapaw.com

In Memoriam

Frankie Jane Powers Cammack (1903-1995)

Elam Allen Campbell (1898-1995)

The idea for this volume came from the Rev. Joe Fort, then pastor of Kingwood United Methodist Church in the Houston suburb of Kingwood, Texas. Rev. Fort suggested that it might be handy to have a small collection of Wesley writings to put in the hands of interested laypersons. I myself had perceived a need for such a collection for the use of my students (in this case to supplement existing collections of John Wesley's Sermons), and so I have developed the following collection of writings from John and Charles Wesley with some introductory comments.

I want to express my gratitude to my wife, Dale Marie, who has diligently worked through these texts to be sure that they conform to the printed versions that have been cited, primarily that of the Jackson edition of the *Works* of John Wesley.

This book is dedicated to the memory of my maternal grandmother, Frankie Jane Powers Cammack (1903-1995) and my paternal grandfather, Elam Allen Campbell (1898-1995). I dedicated my earlier book on *The Religion of the Heart* (1991) to their spouses, who had collaborated in writing a history of St. Luke's United Methodist Church in Beaumont, Texas, and thus foreshadowed my work as an historian of the Methodist tradition. The two to whom this volume is dedicated, however, had no complicity in the writing of Methodist history, and so I take them as models of faithful Methodist laypersons, the folk for whose edification the present work is intended.

CONTENTS

INTRODUCTION

This introduction gives a very brief account of the lives of John and Charles Wesley to show the contexts in which the works included were composed. It then offers some specific advice on reading the works of John and Charles Wesley, and some suggestions for further reading.

The Writings in Their Historical Contexts

John Wesley was born in 1703 in the village of Epworth, Lincolnshire, where his father served as priest of the Anglican (Church of England) parish church. His brother Charles was born in the same village in 1707. The brothers were influenced by their scholarly father and by their independently minded, well educated, and pious mother Susanna (née Annesley) Wesley, along with one older brother and a host of younger sisters. John attended Charterhouse School in London, Charles attended Westminster School in London. Both brothers then proceeded to study for degrees at Oxford University where they were students at Christ Church College. After a conversion to religious seriousness around 1725, the brothers sought ordination to the Anglican priesthood. At about the same time, they began meeting with a group of Oxford students who sought to live a common life emphasizing worship, discipline, and service. John

Early lives of John and Charles Wesley

became a fellow (faculty member) of Lincoln College, Oxford, in 1727.

Following their father's death in 1735, the brothers went to the newly established colony of Georgia in North America, John as a missionary of the Society for the Propagation of the Gospel and Charles as personal secretary to General James Oglethorpe, the founder of the colony. During the Atlantic crossing en route to Georgia, the Wesley brothers met Moravian Christians intent on founding a colony there, and in the colony they would have contact with Moravians and with Lutheran Pietists. Both of these groups emphasized to the Wesley brothers the importance of heartfelt religious faith. The brothers stayed in North America until early 1738, when they returned to England. On board ship returning to England in January 1738, John Wesley wrote out a personal introspection, giving a narrative of his religious life up to that point as a progression through a number of theological and spiritual perspectives (item 1 in this collection).

The Georgia mission (1735-1738)

Back in England in the spring of 1738 and still under the influence of these pietistic Christians, both brothers had profound religious experiences. Charles' experience came on Pentecost Sunday, 21 May 1738, and John's came three days later on Wednesday evening 24 May 1738 at a meeting in Aldersgate Street, London. John Wesley subsequently wrote an account of this experience for his published *Journal* (item 2).

Conversion experiences (1738)

A year later (in 1739) Charles Wesley would write a poem celebrating the anniversary of his conversion experience (item 5). This was published in 1740 and serves as a example of an outpouring of poetic work that flowed from Charles in the years immediately following 1738. A collection published in 1739 included two of his best known hymns: the Christmas hymn that begins "Hark how all the welkin rings" (thankfully revised by George Whitefield to "Hark, the herald angels sing") and the Easter hymn that begins "Christ the Lord is risen to-day" (item 4). Three years later, Charles Wesley would describe the struggles of the soul leading to conversion in a long poem entitled "Wrestling Jacob" (item 7), which many consider to be his poetic masterpiece.

Charles Wesley's verse, 1739-1742

Meanwhile, John Wesley had witnessed George Whitefield preaching in the open air near Bristol in March 1739, and on 2 April of that year John Wesley himself tried open-air preaching or field preaching for the first time. He described his hearing of Whitefield and his own first outdoor preaching in an excerpt from his published *Journal* (item 3).

John Wesley's first field preaching (1739)

When Whitefield left in the summer of 1739 to take up the work that John Wesley had left in Georgia, he left John Wesley in charge of religious societies that Whitefield had organized in Bristol. John and Charles Wesley met for a while with joint Moravian-Anglican societies in London, but by 1740

Organization of Methodist societies, 1739-1743

their followers had departed from these earlier groups, so that by the early 1740s there were societies both in London, Bristol, and elsewhere in the care of the Wesley brothers. In 1743, John and Charles Wesley drew up a set of "General Rules" that functioned as the original charter or covenant laying out terms for membership and participation in their societies (item 8).

John and Charles Wesley together passed through periods in which they emphasized the more distinctive teachings of their own branch of the revival movement and argued against other popular theological teachings. The early 1740s were such a period. John Wesley's sermon on "Christian Perfection" (1741, item 6) is an account of one of the most distinctive Wesleyan teachings, the doctrine of Christian perfection or entire sanctification, the goal of loving God with all of one's being. In 1747 Charles offered a poem on this distinctive Wesleyan teaching. This poem (item 10) begins with the words "Love Divine, all loves excelling" and would become one of the best known of Charles Wesley's hymns in Methodist hymnals, although many Methodists do not realize that its central subject is the doctrine of Christian perfection.

Teaching on the doctrine of Christian perfection in the 1740s

In the early 1740s the Wesleys often argued vociferously against Calvinistic clergy (such as Whitefield) who taught a doctrine of predestination that involved the belief that God had intended only the salvation of a limited

Opposition to the doctrine of predestination in the 1740s

number of those elect or predestined to salvation. Charles Wesley's hymn on "The Great Supper" (1747, item 10) strongly asserts the universal availability of God's grace to all human beings against the teaching of predestination.

In the early 1740s, the Wesleys came into conflict with a peculiar group of London Moravians (peculiar by Moravian as well as Anglican standards) who had insisted that seekers who had not experienced the new birth and the "assurance of pardon" should not partake of such "means of grace" as the Lord's Supper. In 1745 John Wesley responded to this idea in a sermon on "The Means of Grace" (item 9). Two years later Charles Wesley published a collection of hymns which includes the piece mentioned above on "The Great Supper" (item 10). Selected verses from this longer hymn have been used in Methodist hymnals both as hymns that call for the repentance and conversion of sinners and as hymns that celebrate Christ's grace and presence in the sacrament of holy communion.

Teaching about the means of grace in the 1740s

Despite these periods of conflict, the Wesleys sought at other points in their careers to build alliances with others, including the Calvinistic clergy. The year 1749 marked one of these more irenic periods. In this year John Wesley published a sermon on a "Catholic Spirit," (item 11), which makes the case while that Christians should agree on some foundational principles and practices,

Attempts to build relations with other Christians (1749)

they can "think and let think" (those are John Wesley's own words) on matters of "opinions" or "modes of worship." From the same year is John Wesley's "Letter to a Roman Catholic" (item 12), which gives us some insight into the doctrines and attitudes that, in Wesley's view, should have been common to all Christians, Catholic as well as Protestant.

In expressing their most distinctive teachings, the Wesleys not only inveighed against other viewpoints they believed to be dangerous (like the Calvinistic understanding of predestination), but they also laid out a rich and complex understanding of the "way of salvation," that is, what they believed to be the typical path of the spiritual life in three stages: 1) God's grace preparing human beings for salvation (the Wesleys would call this "preventing" grace; later Methodists would call it "prevenient" grace), involving repentance, "awakening" to God's call, and a desire to please God; 2) God's grace pardoning our sins as we are empowered to believe in Jesus Christ (justifying grace); and 3) God's grace leading us to greater and greater holiness (sanctifying grace), culminating in complete love for God (which Methodists sometimes termed "Christian perfection" or "entire sanctification"). John Wesley's sermon on "The Scripture Way of Salvation" (1765, item 13) lays out this pattern in section I of the sermon, defining and describing each of these terms along the way.

Teaching on the "way of salvation" (1765)

The latter years of John Wesley's life were concerned with the future of the Methodist movement. John and Charles Wesley differed very seriously in their visions for the Methodist future. Charles insisted that the Methodists should remain Anglican in every way, including strict obedience to Anglican customs and church law ("canons"). His followers were sometimes described as "Church Methodists," that is, Methodists who elected to remain clearly within the formal structures and laws of the Church of England. After the 1750s, Charles ceased itinerating (traveling the countryside to preach outside of the context of Anglican churches). Although John would never admit to a break with the Church of England and always considered himself to be a priest of that Church, he was willing for the sake of his mission to take steps that were contrary to the formal rules or canons of his Church. Most notably, in response to American independence in the 1770s and the lack of ordained ministers in North America, John Wesley decided in 1784 to ordain clergy who could celebrate baptism and holy communion in North America. This led to the formal organization of an American Methodist church in that year. Charles Wesley disagreed strongly with this move: he wrote a poem to protest it, while John wrote out a letter justifying his reasons for taking this action (item 14).

John Wesley also involved himself in some of the crucial moral issues of his age. He

Provision for a Methodist church in North America (1784)

consistently opposed slavery, and the "General Rules" that he and Charles had drawn up in 1743 (item 8) forbade Methodist people from engaging in the slave trade. The last letter we have from John Wesley was written in 1791 to encourage William Wilberforce's attempts to secure abolition of the slave trade (and eventually the institution of slavery) in British dominions (item 15).

Letter to William Wilberforce on slavery (1791)

By the time John Wesley wrote this letter to Wilberforce, his brother Charles had been dead for three years (he died in 1788). John died six days after writing this letter, on 2 March 1791. John is buried behind the Chapel on City Road, London, and Charles is buried in the consecrated (Anglican) Garden of Rest cemetery at St. Marylebone Church on Marylebone Road, London.

Reading John and Charles Wesley

The writings of John and Charles Wesley offered here are organized in chronological sequence as noted in the brief narrative given above. All the readings given here, with the exception of John Wesley's private self inspection (item 1), are taken from the editions of John and Charles Wesley's works which have been long in the public domain:

Sources of the readings

> Thomas Jackson, ed., *The Works of the Reverend John Wesley, A.M.* (14 vols.; London: Wesleyan Conference Office, 1873). Cited as "Jackson, *Works.*"

George Osborn, ed., *The Poetical
Works of John and Charles Wesley*
(13 vols., London: Wesleyan Conference Office, 1868-1872). Cited as
"Osborn, *Poetical Works*."

These are not by far the most recent and
critical editions of John and Charles Wesley's works, but the fact that their texts are
in the public domain makes them usable
editions for this reader. The other materials,
including this introduction and my introductory comments, are copyrighted, but I
have released them under the terms of a
Creative Commons license (see the reverse
of the title page) which allows the whole
content of this reader to be copied freely so
long as it is copied intact, with all author
and copyright notices preserved.

I have left materials in this collection in
their eighteenth-century forms, including
original titles and British spelling of words.
I have retained verses and expressions that
may give offense to contemporary readers,
and which are consistently removed, for example, in contemporary Methodist hymnals. Charles Wesley's hymn on "Wrestling
Jacob," for example, has the delicate line,
"To me, to all thy bowels move..." which
modern Methodist hymnals change to read,
"To me, to all thy mercies move..." Clearly
the meaning of the expression "bowels
moved" has changed in the last two hundred years. Charles Wesley's hymn "For the
Anniversary Day of One's Conversion" (item
5) has a verse with a racially demeaning im-

Use of historic
forms

age, asserting that when one believes and is born again, Christ will illuminate the believer: in Charles Wesley's image, Christ will "wash the Ethiop white." For appropriate reasons of racial sensitivity, this verse has not been included in Methodist hymnals, even in the text-only version of the poem in the current (1989) *United Methodist Hymnal*, which includes seventeen of the original eighteen verses. I have included it in this collection, however, since this collection gives historical texts in their original language and is not designed (as a hymnal is) to be read or sung as reflecting the consensus of a church.

In the works included here, John and Charles Wesley use a number of English forms that are now archaic. The second-person pronoun "you" in their usage was considered to be formal, and they often address the reader using the second-person singular pronoun "thou" which in their usage was the more informal and "familiar" pronoun ("familiar" meaning the form that would be typically used in a family setting). "Thou" was construed with the corresponding verb forms ending with "-st" or "-est" as in "thou diedst," or "thou readest." The objective form of "thou" was "thee," used as the object of a sentence, the object of a preposition, or as an indirect object. The corresponding second-person plural familiar pronoun was "ye" (in both subjective and objective forms). Third-person singular verb forms (used with a singular noun or

Archaic grammatical forms

the pronouns he, she, it) were used with corresponding verb forms ending in "-th" or "-eth" as in "she loveth" or "he dreameth." Readers will also find some archaic spellings of words, such as "shew" for "show."

We should note some of the particular literary genres employed by the Wesleys. John Wesley kept personal diaries for most of his life after 1725. The diary was a private document, and readers need to realize that John Wesley's *Journal*, unlike his diaries, was written for publication (that's why its title is italicized) and was typically written down months or years after the events described, based on Wesley's memory, his diaries, and his skill as a writer. This collection of Wesley materials includes two excerpts from his published *Journal* (items 2 and 3) and a piece from January 1738 (item 1) that bears a close resemblance to the *Journal*, even though it was not published by John Wesley.

Reading John Wesley's diaries and Journal

The longest pieces in this reader, by far, are four sermons by John Wesley. Readers will readily see that these sermons have very regular structures or outlines which makes them relatively easy to follow despite Wesley's eighteenth-century English. I have added notes leading readers through the structure of the sermons in text boxes in the right-hand margin.

Reading John Wesley's sermons

Modern readers are seldom aware of the "periodic" style in which Wesley and other

The "periodic" style of oral delivery of sermons

preachers of his age would declaim such sermons. Rather than dividing the text into full sentences, the oral performer of these texts divided them into shorter "periods" in which the voice would rise to a strongly emphasized "cadence" consisting typically of one or two emphasized syllables and followed by a pause during which the speaker would breathe. John Wesley sometimes indicates the end of a period by the use of a comma, but in other places he does not indicate periodic breaks in the text, and so the reader has to find them. For example, the sermon on "Christian Perfection" (item 6) begins with the line, "There is scarce any expression in Holy Writ..." which formed a period by itself, with "Holy Writ" the emphasized cadence, followed by a pause before continuing with the sentence. In some cases, however, there are one-syllable cadences and in some places there are "semi-periods" with very brief pauses between them before reaching the end of a longer period. In any case, it is important for readers to try to envision the oral performance of these sermons.

Charles Wesley wrote thousands of poems and hymns throughout his lifetime. Many of these were strictly poems and were not intended to be sung. Others were clearly designed to be sung by a congregation as hymns. In many cases, Methodist churches selected verses from Charles Wesley's longer poems to form smaller hymns. In fact, John Wesley did this with his brother's

Reading Charles Wesley's hymns and poems

poem "For the Anniversary Day of One's Conversion" (1739, item 5), forming the hymn "O, For a Thousand Tongues to Sing."

Suggestions for Further Reading

An important and very readable biography of John Wesley is that of Henry Rack, *Reasonable Enthusiast: John Wesley and the Rise of Methodism* (Philadelphia: Trinity Press International, 1989). Richard Heitzenrater's *John Wesley and the People Called Methodists* (Nashville: Abingdon Press, 1995) offers a critical account of the lives of John and Charles Wesley, intertwined with the development of the Methodist societies that would give rise to Methodist churches.

A seminal study of John Wesley's theology was that of Colin Williams, *John Wesley's Theology Today* (Nashville: Abingdon Press, 1960). Another popular (and short) account of John Wesley's theology was given by Albert C. Outler in *Theology in the Wesleyan Spirit* (Nashville: Tidings, 1975). In more recent decades, these works by Williams and Outler have been supplanted by newer interpretations of John Wesley's theology. Randy Maddox's *Responsible Grace* (Nashville: Abingdon Press/Kingswood Books, 1994) offers a contemporary account of John Wesley's theology in relation to the Christian tradition and in dialogue with contemporary theological issues. Theodore Runyon's *The New Cre-*

ation: John Wesley's Theology Today
(Nashville: Abingdon, 1998) also examines
John Wesley's theology with respect to contemporary issues, especially those raised by
liberation theologies. Kenneth J. Collins's
*The Scripture Way of Salvation: The Heart
of John Wesley's Theology* (Nashville:
Abingdon Press, 1997) offers a carefully nu-
anced account of John Wesley's theology
and spirituality, focusing on the theme of
the "way of salvation," the distinctively
Wesleyan teaching about the way of the
Christian life.

Two works that consider Wesleyan theology
in relationship to the formal doctrinal standards of American Methodist churches are
Scott J. Jones's *United Methodist Doctrine:
The Extreme Center* (Nashville: United
Methodist Publishing House, 2002), which
focuses on doctrine in The United
Methodist Church, and my own somewhat
briefer study of *Methodist Doctrine: The
Essentials* (Nashville: Abingdon Press,
1999), which considers doctrine in a broad-
er range of Methodist denominations.

A standard collection of materials on
Charles Wesley is that edited by John R.
Tyson, *Charles Wesley: A Reader* (New
York: Oxford University Press, 1989). Tyson
also has authored a new biography of
Charles Wesley entitled *Assist Me To Proclaim* (William B. Eerdmans, 2007). A critical new biographical study of Charles Wesley has been offered by Gareth Lloyd,

Charles Wesley and the Struggle for Methodist Identity (Oxford: Oxford University Press, 2007), which focuses on the struggle between John and Charles Wesley over the role of the Methodist movement in relation to the Church of England.

JOHN WESLEY, PRIVATE SELF-INSPECTION
DATED 25 JANUARY 1738

Comment: The following document was written out by
John Wesley in late January 1738 on board ship returning
to England from his journey to Georgia. This document
was written on separate sheets of paper and was neither
part of John Wesley's diaries nor of his published *Journal*,
but bears a strong resemblance to *Journal* entries in which
he looked back on his own life (see the next entry, item 2,
which bears similarities to this document). This is an
account of theological pilgrimage, written in a distressing
period in which John Wesley's hopes for the Georgia
mission had failed and also after a failed relationship with
a young woman in Georgia, Sophia Hopkey. From John
Wesley's careful records of his readings, scholars are able
to reconstruct on some detail the spiritual and theological
pilgrimage he offers here.

This narrative depicts roughly a) John Wesley's own
upbringing (the first two paragraphs), b) his study in
European Protestant (Lutheran and Reformed)
theologians, c) his study of "Caroline" Anglican theologians
(those who, in contention with Puritans had developed a
more Catholic understanding of the Christian faith) and
Non-Jurors (those who broke fellowship with the Church
of England over the legitimacy of the Stuart monarchs, and
who also favored a consistently Catholic interpretation of
Christian faith), d) his study of works on ancient
Christianity that emphasized the model of the primitive
church in the first four centuries, e) his study of mystical
writers, probably under the tutelage of William Law,
although he does not explicitly mention Law here, and

then f) a recognition of problems with the mystical writers.

Source: The document was originally published in Henry Moore's *Life of The Rev'd John Wesley* (1824-1825), 1:342. The version given here has been scanned from Nehemiah Curnock, ed., *The Journal of the Rev. John Wesley, A.M.* (8 vols.; London: Epworth Press, 1909-1919), 1:418-420.

For many years I have been tossed by various winds of doctrine. I asked long ago, 'What must I do to be saved?' The Scripture answered, Keep the commandments, believe, hope, love; follow after these tempers till thou hast fully attained, that is till death; by all those outward works and means which God hath appointed, by walking as Christ walked.

I was early warned against laying, as the Papists do, too much stress on outward works, or on a faith without works; which, as it does not include, so it will never lead to, true hope or charity. Nor am I sensible that to this hour I have laid too much stress on either; having from the very beginning valued both faith, and the means of grace, and good works, not on their own account, but as believing God, who had appointed them, would by them bring me in due time to the mind that was in Christ.

"Papists": a derogatory term for Roman Catholics

But before God's time was come, I fell among some Lutheran and Calvinist authors, whose confused and indigested accounts magnified faith to such an amazing

Study of Continental Protestant theologians

size that it quite hid all the rest of the commandments. I did not then see that this was the natural effect of their overgrown fear of Popery; being so terrified with the cry of merit and good works, that they plunged at once into the other extreme. In this labyrinth I was utterly lost; not being able to find out what the error was, nor yet to reconcile this uncouth hypothesis either with Scripture or common sense.

"Popery": a derogatory term for Catholicism

The English writers, such as Bishop Beveridge, Bishop Taylor, and Mr. Nelson, a little relieved me from these well-meaning, wrong-headed Germans. Their accounts of Christianity I could easily see to be, in the main, consistent both with reason and Scripture. Only when they interpreted Scripture in different ways, I was often much at a loss. And again, there was one thing much insisted on in Scripture—the unity of the Church—which none of them, I thought, clearly explained or strongly inculcate.

Studies in Caroline Anglican theologians and Non-Jurors

But it was not long before Providence brought me to those who showed me a sure rule of interpreting Scripture, viz. *'Consensus veterum: quod ab omnibus, quod ubique, quod semper creditum.'* At the same time they sufficiently insisted upon a due regard to the one Church at all times and in all places.

Studies in ancient Christianity: the Latin quotation (from Vincent of Lérins) means "The consensus of the ancients: that which has been believed by all, everywhere, and always"

Nor was it long before I bent the bow too far the other way: 1. By making antiquity a co-ordinate rather than subordinate rule with

Scripture. 2. By admitting several doubtful writings as undoubted evidences of antiquity. 3. By extending antiquity too far, even to the middle or end of the fourth century. 4. By believing more practices to have been universal in the ancient Church than ever were so. 5. By not considering that the decrees of one Provincial Synod could bind only those provinces whose representatives met therein. 6. By not considering that the most of those decrees were adapted to particular times and occasions; and consequently, when those occasions ceased, must cease to bind even those provinces.

These considerations insensibly stole upon me as I grew acquainted with the Mystic writers, whose noble descriptions of union with God and internal religion made everything else appear mean, flat, and insipid. But in truth they made good works appear so too; yea, and faith itself, and what not? These gave me an entire new view of religion-nothing like any I had before. But, alas! it was nothing like that religion which Christ and His apostles lived and taught. I had a plenary dispensation from all the commands of God: the form ran thus, 'Love is all; all the commands beside are only means of love: you must choose those which you feel are means to you, and use them as long as they are so.' Thus were all the bands burst at once. And though I could never fully come into this, nor contentedly omit what God enjoined; yet, I know not how, I fluctuated between obedience and disobedi-

Studies in mystical theological and spiritual writers

Recognition of problems with mystical writers

ence. I had no heart, no vigour, no zeal in obeying; continually doubting whether I was right or wrong, and never out of perplexities and entanglements. Nor can I at this hour give a distinct account how or when I came a little back toward the right way: only my present sense is this—all the other enemies of Christianity are triflers; the Mystics are the most dangerous of its enemies. They stab it in the vitals; and its most serious professors are most likely to fall by them. May I praise Him who hath snatched me out of this fire likewise, by warning all others that it is set on fire of hell.

JOHN WESLEY, *JOURNAL* ENTRY FOR 24 MAY 1738

Comment: The following passage includes the best known single piece of John Wesley's writings, namely, his account of his Aldersgate Street conversion experience of 24 May 1738. However, most collections of Wesley materials include only paragraphs 13 and 14 of this extended account, and it is important to see these paragraphs in the context of the whole extended passage. In fact, it is the larger context of the "fascicles" or installments in which Wesley originally issued the *Journal* that explains why this experience has been interpreted as a conversion experience: the first published fascicle concludes with John Wesley's admission "that I who went to America to convert others, was never myself converted to God" (*Journal* for 29 January 1738); the second fascicle begins with the events leading up to the Aldersgate Street experience of May 1738. However, it is also the case that John Wesley later added a footnote to his claim that he had not been converted before 1738, and the later footnote questions his earlier implication that he had not been a Christian in any sense before the Aldersgate Street experience. In fact, readers will notice that in the first numbered paragraph below, John Wesley states that "till I was about ten years old I had not sinned away that 'washing of the Holy Ghost' which was given me in baptism," and this indicates his consistent belief that the baptism of infants conveys the grace of regeneration (the new birth in Christ), even if one later "sins away" this grace.

Source: Jackson, *Works*, 1:98-104.

What occurred on *Wednesday*, 24, I think best to relate at large, after premising what may make it the better understood. Let him that cannot receive it ask of the Father of lights, that He would give more light to him and me.

1. I believe, till I was about ten years old I had not sinned away that "washing of the Holy Ghost" which was given me in baptism; having been strictly educated and carefully taught, that I could only be saved "by universal obedience, by keeping all the commandments of God;" in the meaning of which I was diligently instructed. And those instructions, so far as they respected outward duties and sins, I gladly received, and often thought of. But all that was said to me of inward obedience, or holiness, I neither understood nor remembered. So that I was indeed as ignorant of the true meaning of the Law, as I was of the Gospel of Christ.

2. The next six or seven years were spent at school; where, outward restraints being removed, I was much more negligent than before, even of outward duties, and almost continually guilty of outward sins, which I knew to be such, though they were not scandalous in the eye of the world. However, I still read the Scriptures, and said my pray-

Here John Wesley refers to his time at Charterhouse School, London, 1714-1720

ers, morning and evening. And what I now
hoped to be saved by, was,

> 1. Not being so bad as other
> people.

> 2. Having still a kindness for
> religion. And,

> 3. Reading the Bible, going to
> church, and saying my pray-
> ers.

3. Being removed to the University for five
years, I still said my prayers both in public
and in private, and read, with the Scriptures, several other books of religion, especially comments on the New Testament. Yet
I had not all this while so much as a notion
of inward holiness; nay, went on habitually,
and, for the most part, very contentedly, in
some or other known sin: Indeed, with
some intermission and short struggles, especially before and after the holy communion, which I was obliged to receive thrice a
year. I cannot well tell what I hoped to be
saved by now, when I was continually sinning against that little light I had; unless by
those transient fits of what many Divines
taught me to call repentance.

Here John Wesley refers to his time at Christ Church College, Oxford, 1720-1726

4. When I was about twenty-two, my father
pressed me to enter into holy orders. At the
same time, the providence of God directing
me to Kempis's "Christian Pattern," I began
to see, that true religion was seated in the
heart, and that God's law extended to all our
thoughts as well as words and actions. I

1725

was, however, very angry at Kempis, for being too strict; though I read him only in Dean Stanhope's translation. Yet I had frequently much sensible comfort in reading him, such as I was an utter stranger to before: And meeting likewise with a religious friend, which I never had till now, I began to alter the whole form of my conversation, and to set in earnest upon a new life. I set apart an hour or two a day for religious retirement. I communicated every week. I watched against all sin, whether in word or deed. I began to aim at, and pray for, inward holiness. So that now, "doing so much, and living so good a life," I doubted not but I was a good Christian.

5. Removing soon after to another College, I executed a resolution which I was before convinced was of the utmost importance,— shaking off at once all my trifling acquaintance. I began to see more and more the value of time. I applied myself closer to study. I watched more carefully against actual sins; I advised others to be religious, according to that scheme of religion by which I modelled my own life. But meeting now with Mr. Law's "Christian Perfection" and "Serious Call," although I was much offended at many parts of both, yet they convinced me more than ever of the exceeding height and breadth and depth of the law of God. The light flowed in so mightily upon my soul, that every thing appeared in a new view. I cried to God for help, and resolved not to prolong the time of obeying Him as I

John Wesley became a fellow of Lincoln College, Oxford, in 1726

had never done before. And by my continued endeavour to keep His whole law, inward and outward, to the utmost of my
power, I was persuaded that I should be ac-
cepted of Him, and that I was even then in a
state of salvation.

6. In 1730 I began visiting the prisons; assisting the poor and sick in town;and doing
what other good I could, by my presence, or
my little fortune, to the bodies and souls of
all men. To this end I abridged myself of all
superfluities, and many that are called ne-
cessaries of life. I soon became a by-word
for so doing, and I rejoiced that my name
was cast out as evil. The next spring I began
observing the Wednesday and Friday Fasts,
commonly observed in the ancient Church;
tasting no food till three in the afternoon.
And now I knew not how to go any farther. I
diligently strove against all sin. I omitted no
sort of self-denial which I thought lawful: I
carefully used, both in public and in private,
all the means of grace at all opportunities. I
omitted no occasion of doing good: I for
that reason suffered evil. And all this I knew
to be nothing, unless as it was directed toward inward holiness. Accordingly this, the
image of God, was what I aimed at in all, by
doing his will, not my own. Yet when, after
continuing some years in this course, I ap-
prehended myself to be near death, I could
not find that all this gave me any comfort,
or any assurance of acceptance with God. At
this I was then not a little surprised; not
imagining I had been all this time building

on the sand, nor considering that "other foundation can no man lay, than that which is laid" by God, "even Christ Jesus."

7. Soon after, a contemplative man convinced me still more than I was convinced before, that outward works are nothing, being alone; and in several conversations instructed me, how to pursue inward holiness, or a union of the soul with God. But even of his instructions (though I then received them as the words of God) I cannot but now observe, 1. That he spoke so incautiously against trusting in outward works, that he discouraged me from doing them at all. 2. That he recommended (as it were, to supply what was wanting in them) *mental prayer*, and the like exercises, as the most effectual means of purifying the soul, and uniting it with God. Now these were, in truth, as much my own works as visiting the sick or clothing the naked; and the union with God thus pursued, was as really my own righteousness, as any I had before pursued under another name.

The "contemplative man" John Wesley refers to here was probably the spiritual writer William Law

8. In this refined way of trusting to my own works and my own righteousness, (so zealously inculcated by the mystic writers,) I dragged on heavily, finding no comfort or help therein, till the time of my leaving England. On shipboard, however, I was again active in outward works; where it pleased God of his free mercy to give me twenty-six of the Moravian brethren for companions, who endeavoured to show me "a more ex-

John Wesley's voyage to Georgia in late 1735

cellent way." But I understood it not at first. I was too learned and too wise. So that it seemed foolishness unto me. And I continued preaching, and following after, and trusting in, that righteousness whereby no flesh can be justified.

9. All the time I was at Savannah I was thus beating the air. Being ignorant of the righteousness of Christ, which, by a living faith in Him, bringeth salvation "to every one that believeth," I sought to establish my own righteousness; and so laboured in the fire all my days. I was now properly "under the law;" I knew that "the law" of God was "spiritual; I consented to it that it was good." Yea, "I delighted in it, after the inner man." Yet was I "carnal, sold under sin." Everyday was I constrained to cry out, "What I do, I allow not: For what I would, I do not; but what I hate, that I do. To will is" indeed "present with me: But how to perform that which is good, I find not. For the good which I would, I do not; but the evil which I would not, that I do. I find a law, that when I would do good, evil is present with me:" Even "the law in my members, warring against the law of my mind," and still "bringing me into captivity to the law of sin."

10. In this vile, abject state of bondage to sin, I was indeed fighting continually, but not conquering. Before, I had willingly served sin; now it was unwillingly; but still I served it. I fell, and rose, and fell again.

Sometimes I was overcome, and in heaviness: Sometimes I overcame, and was in joy. For as in the former state I had some foretastes of the terrors of the law, so had I in this, of the comforts of the Gospel. During this whole struggle between nature and grace, which had now continued above ten years, I had many remarkable returns to prayer; especially when I was in trouble: I had many sensible comforts; which are indeed no other than short anticipations of the life of faith. But I was still "under the law," not "under grace:" (The state most who are called Christians are content to live and die in:) For I was only striving with, not freed from, sin: Neither had I the witness of the Spirit with my spirit, and indeed could not; for I "sought it not by faith, but as it were by the works of the law."

11. In my return to England, January, 1738, being in imminent danger of death, and very uneasy on that account, I was strongly convinced that the cause of that uneasiness was unbelief; and that the gaining a true, living faith was the "one thing needful" for me. But still I fixed not this faith on its right object: I meant only faith in God, not faith in or through Christ. Again, I knew not that I was wholly void of this faith; but only thought, I had not enough of it. So that when Peter Böhler, whom God prepared for me as soon as I came to London, affirmed of true faith in Christ, (which is but one,) that it had those two fruits inseparably attending it, "Dominion over sin, and constant Peace

John Wesley's return to England in early 1738

from a sense of forgiveness," I was quite amazed, and looked upon it as a new Gospel. If this was so, it was clear I had not faith. But I was not willing to be convinced of this. Therefore, I disputed with all my might, and laboured to prove that faith might be where these were not; especially where the sense of forgiveness was not: For all the Scriptures relating to this I had been long since taught to construe away; and to call all Presbyterians who spoke otherwise. Besides, I well saw, no one could, in the nature of things, have such a sense of forgiveness, and not feel it. But I felt it not. If then there was no faith without this, all my pretensions to faith dropped at once.

12. When I met Peter Böhler again, he consented to put the dispute upon the issue which I desired, namely, Scripture and experience. I first consulted the Scripture. But when I set aside the glosses of men, and simply considered the words of God, comparing them together, endeavouring to illustrate the obscure by the plainer passages; I found they all made against me, and was forced to retreat to my last hold, "that experience would never agree with the *literal interpretation* of those scriptures. Nor could I therefore allow it to be true, till I found some living witnesses of it." He replied, he could show me such at any time; if I desired it, the next day. And accordingly, the next day he came again with three others, all of whom testified, of their own personal experience, that a true living faith in

Christ is inseparable from a sense of pardon
for all past, and freedom from all present,
sins. They added with one mouth, that this
faith was the gift, the free gift of God; and
that he would surely bestow it upon every
soul who earnestly and perseveringly sought
it. I was now thoroughly convinced; and, by
the grace of God, I resolved to seek it unto
the end, 1. By absolutely renouncing all de-
pendence, in whole or in part, upon *my
own* works or righteousness; on which I had
really grounded my hope of salvation,
though I knew it not, from my youth up. 2.
By adding to the constant use of all the other means of grace, continual prayer for this
very thing, justifying, saving faith, a full reliance on the blood of Christ shed for *me*; a
trust in Him, as *my* Christ, as *my* sole justification, sanctification, and redemption.

13. I continued thus to seek it, (though with
strange indifference, dulness, and coldness,
and unusually frequent relapses into sin,)
till Wednesday, May 24. I think it was about
five this morning, that I opened my Testament on those words, τὰ μέγιστα ἡμῖν
καὶ τίμια ἐπαγγέλματα δεδώρηται ἵνα
γένεσθε θείας κοινοινοὶ φύσεως.
"There are given unto us exceeding great
and precious promises, even that ye should
be partakers of the divine nature." (2 Peter
1:4.) Just as I went out, I opened it again on
those words, "Thou art not far from the
kingdom of God." In the afternoon I was
asked to go to St. Paul's. The anthem was,
"Out of the deep have I called unto thee, O

Lord: Lord, hear my voice. O let thine ears consider well the voice of my complaint. If thou, Lord, wilt be extreme to mark what is done amiss, O Lord, who may abide it? For there is mercy with thee; therefore shalt thou be feared. O Israel, trust in the Lord: For with the Lord there is mercy, and with him is plenteous redemption. And He shall redeem Israel from all his sins."

14. In the evening I went very unwillingly to a society in Aldersgate-Street, where one was reading Luther's preface to the Epistle to the Romans. About a quarter before nine, while he was describing the change which God works in the heart through faith in Christ, I felt my heart strangely warmed. I felt I did trust in Christ, Christ alone for salvation: And an assurance was given me, that he had taken away *my* sins, even *mine*, and saved *me* from the law of sin and death.

15. I began to pray with all my might for those who had in a more especial manner despitefully used me and persecuted me. I then testified openly to all there, what I now first felt in my heart. But it was not long before the enemy suggested, "This cannot be faith; for where is thy joy?" Then was I taught, that peace and victory over sin are essential to faith in the Captain of our salvation: But that, as to the transports of joy that usually attend the beginning of it, especially in those who have mourned deeply, God sometimes giveth, sometimes withhol-

deth them, according to the counsels of his
own will.

16. After my return home, I was much buf-
feted with temptations; but cried out, and
they fled away. They returned again and
again. I as often lifted up my eyes, and He
"sent me help from his holy place." And
herein I found the difference between this
and my former state chiefly consisted. I was
striving, yea, fighting with all my might under the law, as well as under grace. But then
I was sometimes, if not often, conquered;
now, I was always conqueror.

17. Thur. 25.—The moment I awaked, "Jesus, Master," was in my heart and in my
mouth; and I found all my strength lay in
keeping my eye fixed upon him, and my soul
waiting on him continually. Being again at
St. Paul's in the afternoon, I could taste the
good word of God in the anthem, which
began, "My song shall be always of the loving kindness of the Lord: With my mouth
will I ever be showing forth thy truth from
one generation to another." Yet the enemy
injected a fear, "If thou dost believe, why is
there not a more sensible change?" I
answered, (yet not I,) "That I know not. But
this I know, I have 'now peace with God.'
And I sin not today, and Jesus my Master
has forbid me to take thought for the morrow."

18. "But is not any sort of fear," continued
the tempter, "a proof that thou dost not believe?" I desired my Master to answer for

me; and opened his Book upon those words
of St. Paul, "Without were fightings, within
were fears." Then, inferred I, well may fears
be within me; but I must go on, and tread
them under my feet.

JOHN WESLEY, *JOURNAL* ENTRIES
FOR 31 MARCH – 2 APRIL 1739

Comment: The following entries from John Wesley's *Journal* depict the beginning of his open-air preaching. As he states here, he had witnessed George Whitefield doing the same, and Whitefield had been in communication with the Welsh itinerant Howell Harris, who had begun preaching outdoors from the winter or spring of 1736. The Act of Toleration of 1689 provided that worship should be conducted in an Anglican church or chapel or in a registered dissenting place of worship. Outdoor preaching could be and was seen as contradicting this foundational law for eighteenth-century England, and John Wesley was within a few days upbraided by the Bishop of Bristol, who objected to the practice on the grounds of the Act of Toleration.

Source: Jackson, *Works*, 1:185.

Saturday, 31. In the evening I reached Bristol, and met Mr. Whitefield there. I could scarce reconcile myself at first to this strange way of preaching in the fields, of which he set me an example on Sunday; having been all my life (till very lately) so tenacious of every point relating to decency and order, that I should have thought the saving of souls almost a sin, if it had not been done in a church.

APRIL 1.—In the evening (Mr. Whitefield being gone) I begun expounding our Lord's

Sermon on the Mount, (one pretty remarkable precedent of field-preaching, though I suppose there were churches at that time also,) to a little society which was accustomed to meet once or twice a week in Nicholas-Street.

Mon. 2.—At four in the afternoon, I submitted to be more vile, and proclaimed in the highways the glad tidings of salvation, speaking from a little eminence in a ground adjoining to the city, to about three thousand people. The scripture on which I spoke was this, (is it possible any one should be ignorant, that it is fulfilled in every true Minister of Christ?) "The Spirit of the Lord is upon me, because he hath anointed me to preach the Gospel to the poor. He hath sent me to heal the brokenhearted; to preach deliverance to the captives, and recovery of sight to the blind: To set at liberty them that are bruised, to proclaim the acceptable year of the Lord."

ITEM 4:

CHARLES WESLEY, "HYMN FOR CHRISTMAS-DAY" AND "HYMN FOR EASTER-DAY" (1739)

Comment: The two hymns given here are among the best known of Charles Wesley's hymns. They were both published in a collection of *Hymns and Sacred Poems* (1739), which lists both John and Charles Wesley as authors, although it is doubted whether John actually composed any of the poems and hymns in the collection and these two have always been attributed to Charles. Within this large collection of hymns and poems, these two appear within a liturgical sequence of five hymns: for Christmas day, Epiphany, Easter Sunday, Ascension day, and Pentecost. Later, Charles Wesley would compose a series of whole collections of hymns for four of these celebrations in the Christian liturgical year: *Hymns on the Nativity* (1745), *Hymns for our Lord's Resurrection* (1746), *Hymns for Ascension-Day* (1746), and *Hymns of Petition and Thanksgiving for the Promise of the Father* subtitled *Hymns for Whitsunday* (1746; "Whitsunday" is a British term for Pentecost Sunday). The Anglo-Saxon term "welkin" in the first line below denotes the arc of the heavens; it was George Whitefield who changed this first line to "Hark, the herald angels sing." (Thanks, George.)

Source: These hymns were first published in *Hymns and Sacred Poems* (1739, pp. 206-208, 209-211). The versions cited here are from Osborn, *Poetical Works*, 1:183-184, 185-186.

Hymn for Christmas-Day

Hark how all the welkin rings,
"Glory to the King of kings,
Peace on earth, and mercy mild,
God and sinners reconciled!"

Joyful, all ye nations, rise,
Join the triumph of the skies;
Universal Nature, say,
"Christ the Lord is born to-day!"

Christ, by highest heaven adored,
Christ, the everlasting Lord,
Late in time behold Him come,
Offspring of a virgin's womb.

Veil'd in flesh, the Godhead see,
Hail the' Incarnate Deity!
Pleased as man with men to' appear
Jesus, our Immanuel here!

Hail the heavenly Prince of Peace!
Hail the Sun of Righteousness!
Light and life to all He brings,
Risen with healing in His wings.

Mild He lays His glory by,
Born—that man no more may die,
Born—to raise the sons of earth,
Born—to give them second birth.

Come, Desire of Nations, come,
Fix in us Thy humble home;

Rise, the woman's conquering Seed,
Bruise in us the serpent's head.

Now display Thy saving power,
Ruin'd nature now restore;
Now in mystic union join
Thine to ours, and ours to Thine.

Adam's likeness, Lord, efface,
Stamp Thy image in its place;
Second Adam from above,
Reinstate us in Thy love.

Let us Thee, though lost, regain,
Thee, the Life, the Inner Man:
O! to all Thyself impart,
Form'd in each believing heart.

Hymn for Easter-Day

"Christ the Lord is risen to-day,"
Sons of men and angels say!
Raise your joys and triumphs high;
Sing, ye heavens; and, earth, reply.

Love's redeeming work is done,
Fought the fight, the battle won:
Lo! our Sun's eclipse is o'er;
Lo! He sets in blood no more.

Vain the stone, the watch, the seal;
Christ has burst the gates of hell!
Death in vain forbids His rise:
Christ has open'd paradise!

Lives again our glorious King:
Where, O Death, is now thy sting?
Dying once, He all doth save:
Where thy victory, O Grave?

Soar we now, where Christ has led?
Following our exalted Head,
Made like Him, like Him we rise,
Ours the cross, the grave, the skies!

What though once we perish'd all,
Partners in our parent's fall?
Second life we all receive,
In our Heavenly Adam live.

Risen with Him, we upward move;
Still we seek the things above;
Still pursue, and kiss the Son
Seated on His Father's throne:

Scarce on earth a thought bestow,
Dead to all we leave below;
Heaven our aim, and loved abode,
Hid our life with Christ in God!

Hid; till Christ, our Life, appear,
Glorious in His members here:
Join'd to Him, we then shall shine
All immortal, all Divine!

Hail, the Lord of earth and heaven!
Praise to Thee by both be given:
Thee we greet triumphant now;
Hail, the Resurrection Thou!

King of glory, Soul of bliss,
Everlasting life is this,
Thee to know, Thy power to prove,
Thus to sing, and thus to love!

CHARLES WESLEY,
POEM "FOR THE ANNIVERSARY DAY
OF ONE'S CONVERSION" (1739)

Comment: The following poem includes the verses that would be used in 1780 by John Wesley to form the shorter hymn "O, For a Thousand Tongues to Sing," traditionally the first hymn in Methodist hymnals. The poem was written by Charles Wesley in 1739 to celebrate the first anniversary of his own conversion experience, which had occurred on May 21, 1738, three days ahead of his brother's Aldersgate Street experience. Although six or seven of the verses are well known to Methodist people, some of the other verses (like "Harlots, and publicans, and thieves/In holy triumph join") might be found surprising by a pious Methodist congregation.

Source: The poem was originally published in *Hymns and Sacred Poems* (1740, pp. 120-123). The version cited here is from Osborn, *Poetical Works*, 1:299-301.

For the Anniversary Day of One's Conversion

Glory to God, and praise, and love
Be ever, ever given,
By saints below, and saints above,
The church in earth and heaven.

On this glad day the glorious Sun
Of Righteousness arose;
On my benighted soul He shone,
And fill'd it with repose.

Sudden expired the legal strife;
'Twas then I ceased to grieve;
My second, real, living life
I then began to live.

Then with my heart I first believed,
Believed with faith Divine;
Power with the Holy Ghost received
To call the Saviour mine.

I felt my Lord's atoning blood
Close to my soul applied;
Me, me He loved—the Son of God
For me, for me He died!

I found, and own'd His promise true,
Ascertain'd of my part;
My pardon pass'd in heaven I knew,
When written on my heart.

O for a thousand tongues to sing
My dear Redeemer's praise!
The glories of my God and King,
The triumphs of His grace.

My gracious Master, and my God,
Assist me to proclaim,
To spread through all the earth abroad
The honours of Thy name.

Jesus, the name that charms our fears,
That bids our sorrows cease;
'Tis music in the sinner's ears,
'Tis life, and health, and peace!

He breaks the power of cancell'd sin,
He sets the prisoner free;
His blood can make the foulest clean,
His blood avail'd for me.

He speaks; and, listening to His voice,
New life the dead receive,
The mournful, broken hearts rejoice,
The humble poor believe.

Hear Him, ye deaf; His praise, ye dumb,
Your loosen'd tongues employ;
Ye blind, behold your Saviour come;
And leap, ye lame, for joy.

Look unto Him, ye nations; own
Your God, ye fallen race!
Look, and be saved through faith alone;
Be justified by grace!

See all your sins on Jesus laid;
The Lamb of God was slain,
His soul was once an offering made
For every soul of man.

Harlots, and publicans, and thieves
In holy triumph join;
Saved is the sinner that believes
From crimes as great as mine.

Murderers, and all ye hellish crew,
Ye sons of lust and pride,
Believe the Saviour died for you;
For me the Saviour died.

Awake from guilty nature's sleep,
And Christ shall give you light,
Cast all your sins into the deep,
And wash the Ethiop white.

With me, your chief, you then shall know,
Shall feel your sins forgiven;
Anticipate your heaven below,
And own that love is heaven.

ITEM 6:

JOHN WESLEY,
SERMON ON "CHRISTIAN PERFECTION" (1741)

Comment: Perhaps the most distinctive and controversial aspect of John Wesley's theology and spirituality was his claim that by divine grace Christians could love God completely and in this sense they could cease sinning, since sin implies lack of love for God. Wesley did not hesitate to utilize the biblical term "perfection" (Matthew 5:48 as well as the passage from Philippians that is the text of the following sermon) to describe the realization of the Great Commandment, "You shall love the Lord your God with all your heart, and with all your soul, and with all your mind" (Deuteronomy 6:4, Matthew 22:37, etc.).

Source: Jackson, *Works*, 6:1-19.

"Not as though I had already attained, either were already perfect." Phil. iii. 12.

1. THERE is scarce any expression in Holy Writ which has given more offence than this. The word *perfect* is what many cannot bear. The very sound of it is an abomination to them; and whosoever *preaches perfection* (as the phrase is,) that is, asserts that it is attainable in this life, runs great hazard of being accounted by them worse than a heathen man or a publican.

Introduction

2. And hence some have advised, wholly to lay aside the use of those expressions; "be-

cause they have given so great offence." But are they not found in the oracles of God? If so, by what authority can any Messenger of God lay them aside, even though all men should be offended? We have not so learned Christ; neither may we thus give place to the devil. Whatsoever God hath spoken that will we speak, whether men will hear, or whether they will forbear; knowing that then alone can any Minister of Christ be "pure from the blood of all men," when he hath "not shunned to declare unto them all the counsel of God."

3. We may not, therefore, lay these expressions aside, seeing they are the words of God, and not of man. But we may and ought to explain the meaning of them, that those who are sincere of heart may not err to the right hand or to the left, from the mark of the prize of their high calling. And this is the more needful to be done because in the verse already repeated the Apostle speaks of himself as not perfect: "Not," saith he, "as though I were already perfect." And yet immediately after, in the fifteenth verse, he speaks of himself, yea, and many others, as perfect: "Let us," saith he, "as many as be perfect, be thus minded."

4. In order, therefore, to remove the difficulty arising from this seeming contradiction, as well as to give light to them who are pressing forward to the mark, and that those who are lame be not turned out of the way, I shall endeavour to show,

First, in what sense Christians *are not*; and,

Secondly, In what sense they *are, perfect*.

I. 1. In the first place I shall endeavour to show, in what sense Christians are *not perfect*. And both from experience and Scripture it appears, First, that they are not perfect in knowledge: they are not so perfect in this life as to be free from ignorance. They know, it may be, in common with other men, many things relating to the present world; and they know, with regard to the world to come, the general truths which God hath revealed. They know, likewise, (what the natural man receiveth not, for these things are spiritually discerned,) "what manner of love" it is wherewith "the Father" hath loved them, "that they should be called the sons of God." They know the mighty working of his Spirit in their hearts; and the wisdom of his providence, directing all their paths, and causing all things to work together for their good. Yea, they know in every circumstance of life what the Lord requireth of them, and how to keep a conscience void of offence both toward God and toward man.

I. The senses in which Christians cannot expect to be perfect

They cannot expect to be free from ignorance

2. But innumerable are the things which they know not. Touching the Almighty himself, they cannot search him out to perfection. "Lo, these are but a part of his ways; but the thunder of his power who can understand?" They cannot understand, I will

not say, how "there are Three that bear record in heaven, the Father, the Son, and the
Holy Spirit, and these three are one;" or
how the eternal Son of God "took upon himself the form of a servant;"—but not any one
attribute, not any one circumstance of the
divine nature. Neither is it for them to know
the times and seasons when God will work
his great works upon the earth; no, not even
those which he hath in part revealed by his
servants and Prophets since the world
began. Much less do they know when God,
having "accomplished the number of his
elect, will hasten his kingdom;" when "the
heavens shall pass away with a great noise,
and the elements shall melt with fervent
heat."

3. They know not the reasons even of many
of his present dispensations with the sons of
men; but are constrained to rest here, –
Though "clouds and darkness are round
about him, righteousness and judgement
are the habitation of his seat." Yea, often
with regard to his dealings with themselves,
doth their Lord say unto them, "What I do,
thou knowest not now; but thou shalt know
hereafter." And how little do they know of
what is ever before them, of even the visible
works of his hands!—how "he spreadeth the
north over the empty place, and hangeth the
earth upon nothing?" how he unites all the
parts of this vast machine by a secret chain
which cannot be broken? So great is the ignorance, so very little the knowledge, of
even the best of men!

4. No one, then, is so perfect in this life, as to be free from ignorance. Nor, Secondly, from mistake; which indeed is almost an unavoidable consequence of it; seeing those who "know but in part" are ever liable to err touching the things which they know not. It is true, the children of God do not mistake as to the things essential to salvation: They do not "put darkness for light, or light for darkness;" neither "seek death in the error of their life." For they are "taught of God;" and the way which he teaches them, the way of holiness, is so plain, that "the wayfaring man, though a fool, need not err therein." But in things unessential to salvation they do err, and that frequently. The best and wisest of men are frequently mistaken even with regard to facts; believing those things not to have been which really were, or those to have been done which were not. Or, suppose they are not mistaken as to the fact itself, they may be with regard to its circumstances; believing them, or many of them, to have been quite different from what, in truth, they were. And hence cannot but arise many farther mistakes. Hence they may believe either past or present actions which were or are evil, to be good; and such as were or are good, to be evil. Hence also they may judge not according to truth with regard to the characters of men; and that, not only by supposing good men to be better, or wicked men to be worse, than they are, but by believing them to have been or to be good men, who were or are very wicked; or

> They cannot expect to be free from mistakes

perhaps those to have been or to be wicked men, who were or are holy and unreprovable.

5. Nay, with regard to the Holy Scriptures themselves, as careful as they are to avoid it, the best of men are liable to mistake, and do mistake day by day; especially with respect to those parts thereof which less immediately relate to practice. Hence, even the children of God are not agreed as to the interpretation of many places in holy writ: Nor is their difference of opinion any proof that they are not the children of God on either side; but it is a proof that we are no more to expect any living man to be infallible than to be omniscient.

6. If it be objected to what has been observed under this and the preceding head, that St. John, speaking to his brethren in the faith says, "Ye have an unction from the Holy One, and ye know all things:" (1 John ii. 20:) The answer is plain: "Ye know all things that are needful for your souls' health." That the Apostle never designed to extend this farther, that he could not speak it in an absolute sense, is clear, First from hence;—that otherwise he would describe the disciple as "above his Master;" seeing Christ himself, as man, knew not all things: "Of that hour," saith he, "knoweth no man; no, not the Son, but the Father only." It is clear, Secondly, from the Apostle's own words that follow: "These things have I written unto you concerning them that de-

ceive you;" as well as from his frequently repeated caution, "Let no man deceive you;"
which had been altogether needless, had not
those very persons who had that unction
from the Holy One been liable, not to ignorance only, but to mistake also.

7. Even Christians, therefore, are not *so* perfect as to be free either from ignorance or
error: We may, Thirdly, add, nor from infirmities.—Only let us take care to understand this word aright: Only let us not give
that soft title to known sins, as the manner
of some is. So, one man tells us, "Every man
has his infirmity, and mine is drunkenness;"
Another has the infirmity of uncleanness;
another of taking God's holy name in vain;
and yet another has the infirmity of calling
his brother, "Thou fool," or returning "railing for railing." It is plain that all you who
thus speak, if ye repent not, shall, with your
infirmities, go quick into hell! But I mean
hereby, not only those which are properly
termed *bodily infirmities*, but all those inward or outward imperfections which are
not of a moral nature. Such are the weakness or slowness of understanding, dulness
or confusedness of apprehension, incoher-
ency of thought, irregular quickness or
heaviness of imagination. Such (to mention
no more of this kind) is the want of a ready
or of a retentive memory. Such, in another
kind, are those which are commonly, in
some measure, consequent upon these;
namely, slowness of speech, impropriety of
language, ungracefulness of pronunciation;

They cannot expect to
be free from infirmities

to which one might add a thousand nameless defects, either in conversation or behaviour. These are the infirmities which are found in the best of men, in a larger or smaller proportion. And from these none can hope to be perfectly freed, till the spirit returns to God that gave it.

8. Nor can we expect, till then, to be wholly free from temptation. Such perfection belongeth not to this life. It is true, there are those who, being given up to work all uncleanness with greediness, scarce perceive the temptations which they resist not; and so seem to be without temptation. There are also many whom the wise enemy of souls, seeing to be fast asleep in the dead form of godliness, will not tempt to gross sin, lest they should awake before they drop into everlasting burnings. I know there are also children of God who, being now justified freely, having found redemption in the blood of Christ, for the present feel no temptation. God hath said to their enemies, "Touch not mine anointed, and do my children no harm." And for this season, it may be for weeks or months, he causeth them to ride on high places he beareth them as on eagles' wings, above all the fiery darts of the wicked one. But this state will not last always; as we may learn from that single consideration,—that the Son of God himself, in the days of his flesh, was tempted even to the end of his life. Therefore, so let his servant expect to be; for "it is enough that he be as his Master."

They cannot expect to be free from temptation

9. Christian perfection, therefore, does not imply (as some men seem to have imagined) an exemption either from ignorance, or mistake, or infirmities or temptations. Indeed, it is only another term for holiness. They are two names for the same thing. Thus, every one that is holy is, in the Scripture sense, perfect. Yet we may, Lastly, observe, that neither in this respect is there any absolute perfection on earth. There is no *perfection of degrees*, as it is termed; none which does not admit of a continual increase. So that how much soever any man hath attained, or in how high a degree soever he is perfect, he hath still need to "grow in grace," and daily to advance in the knowledge and love of God his Saviour.

II. 1. In what sense, then, are Christians perfect? This is what I shall endeavour, in the Second place, to show. But it should be premised, that there are several stages in Christian life, as in natural;- some of the children of God being but new-born babes; others having attained to more maturity. And accordingly St. John, in his first Epistle, (1 John ii. 12, &c.,) applies himself severally to those he terms little children, those he styles young men, and those whom he entitles fathers. "I write unto you, little children," saith the Apostle, "because your sins are forgiven you:" Because thus far you have attained,—being "justified freely," you "have peace with God, through Jesus Christ." "I write unto you, young men, because ye have overcome the wicked one;" or

II. The senses in which Christians *can* expect to be made perfect

(as he afterwards addeth,) "because ye are strong, and the word of God abideth in you." Ye have quenched the fiery darts of the wicked one, the doubts and fears wherewith he disturbed your first peace; and the witness of God, that your sins are forgiven, now abideth in your heart. "I write unto you, fathers, because ye have known him that is from the beginning." Ye have known both the Father and the Son and the Spirit of Christ, in your inmost soul. Ye are "perfect men," being grown up "to the measure of the stature of the fulness of Christ."

2. It is of these chiefly I speak in the latter part of this discourse: For these only are perfect Christians. But even babes in Christ are in such a sense perfect, or born of God, (an expression taken also in divers senses,) as, First, not to commit sin. If any doubt of this privilege of the sons of God, the question is not to be decided by abstract reasonings, which may be drawn out into an endless length, and leave the point just as it was before. Neither is it to be determined by the experience of this or that particular person. Many may suppose they do not commit sin, when they do; but this proves nothing either way. To the law and to the testimony we appeal. "Let God be true, and every man a liar." By his Word will we abide, and that alone. Hereby we ought to be judged.

3. Now the Word of God plainly declares, that even those who are justified, who are born again in the lowest sense, "do not con-

They can expect to be made free from sin

tinue in sin;" that they cannot "live any longer therein;" (Rom. vi. 1, 2;) that they are "planted together in the likeness of the death" of Christ; (verse 5;) that their "old man is crucified with him," the body of sin being destroyed, so that henceforth they do not serve sin; that being dead with Christ, they are free from sin; (verses 6, 7;) that they are "dead unto sin, and alive unto God;" (verse 11;) that "sin hath no more dominion over them," who are "not under the law, but under grace;" but that these, "being free from sin, are become the servants of righteousness." (verses 14, 18)

4. The very least which can be implied in these words, is, that the persons spoken of therein, namely, all real Christians, or believers in Christ, are made free from outward sin. And the same freedom, which St. Paul here expresses in such variety of phrases, St. Peter expresses in that one: (1 Pet. iv. 1, 2:) "He that hath suffered in the flesh hath ceased from sin,—that he no longer should live to the desires of men, but to the will of God." For this *ceasing from sin*, if it be interpreted in the lowest sense, as regarding only the outward behaviour, must denote the ceasing from the outward act, from any outward transgression of the law.

5 . But most express are the well-known words of St. John, in the third chapter of his First Epistle, verse 8, &c.: "He that committeth sin is of the devil; for the devil sinneth

from the beginning. For this purpose the Son of God was manifested, that he might destroy the works of the devil. Whosoever is born of God doth not commit sin; for his seed remaineth in him: And he cannot sin because he is born of God." And those in the fifth: (verse 18:) "We know that whosoever is born of God sinneth not; but he that is begotten of God keepeth himself, and that wicked one toucheth him not."

6. Indeed it is said, this means only, He sinneth not *wilfully*; or he doth not commit sin *habitually*; or, *not as other men do*; or, *not as he did before*. But by whom is this said? By St. John? No. There is no such word in the text; nor in the whole chapter; nor in all his Epistle; nor in any part of his writings whatsoever. Why then, the best way to answer a bold assertion is simply to deny it. And if any man can prove it from the Word of God, let him bring forth his strong reasons.

7. And a sort of reason there is, which has been frequently brought to support these strange assertions, drawn from the examples recorded in the Word of God: "What!" say they, "did not Abraham himself commit sin,—prevaricating, and denying his wife? Did not Moses commit sin, when he provoked God at the waters of strife? Nay, to produce one for all, did not even David, 'the man after God's own heart,' commit sin, in the matter of Uriah the Hittite; even murder and adultery?" It is most sure he

did. All this is true. But what is it you would
infer from hence? It may be granted, First,
that David, in the general course of his life,
was one of the holiest men among the Jews;
and, Secondly, that the holiest men among
the Jews did sometimes commit sin. But if
you would hence infer, that all Christians do
and must commit sin as long as they live;
this consequence *we* utterly deny: It will
never follow from those premises.

8. Those who argue thus, seem never to
have considered that declaration of our
Lord: (Matt. xi. 11:) "Verily I say unto you,
Among them that are born of women there
hath not risen a greater than John the
Baptist: Notwithstanding he that is least in
the kingdom of heaven is greater than he." I
fear, indeed, there are some who have imagined "the kingdom of heaven," here, to
mean the kingdom of glory; as if the Son of
God had just discovered to us, that the least
glorified saint in heaven is greater than any
man upon earth! To mention this is sufficiently to refute it. There can, therefore, no
doubt be made, but "the kingdom of
heaven," here, (as in the following verse,
where it is said to be taken by force.) or,
"the kingdom of God," as St. Luke expresses
it,—is that kingdom of God on earth whereunto all true believers in Christ, all real
Christians, belong. In these words, then,
our Lord declares two things: First, that before his coming in the flesh, among all the
children of men there had not been one
greater than John the Baptist; whence it

evidently follows, that neither Abraham, David, nor any Jew was greater than John. Our Lord, Secondly, declares that he which is least in the kingdom of God (in that kingdom which he came to set up on earth, and which the violent now began to take by force) is greater than he:—Not a greater Prophet as some have interpreted the word; for this is palpably false in fact; but greater in the grace of God, and the knowledge of our Lord Jesus Christ. Therefore, we cannot measure the privileges of real Christians by those formerly given to the Jews. Their "ministration," (or dispensation,) we allow "was glorious;" but ours "exceeds in glory." So that whosoever would bring down the Christian dispensation to the Jewish standard, whosoever gleans up the examples of weakness, recorded in the Law and the Prophets, and thence infers that they who have "put on Christ" are endued with no greater strength, doth greatly err, neither "knowing the Scriptures, nor the power of God."

9. "But are there not assertions in Scripture which prove the same thing, if it cannot be inferred from those examples? Does not the Scripture say expressly, "Even a just man sinneth seven times a day?" I answer, No. The Scripture says no such thing. There is no such text in all the Bible. That which seems to be intended is the sixteenth verse of the twenty-fourth chapter of the Proverbs; the words of which are these: "A just man falleth seven times, and riseth up

again." But this is quite another thing. For, First, the words "a day" are not in the text. So that if a just man falls seven times in his life, it is as much as is affirmed here. Secondly, here is no mention of *falling into sin* at all; what is here mentioned is *falling into temporal affliction*. This plainly appears from the verse before, the words of which are these: "Lay not wait, O wicked man, against the dwelling of the righteous; spoil not his resting place." It follows, "For a just man falleth seven times, and riseth up again; but the wicked shall fall into mischief." As if he had said, "God will deliver him out of his trouble; but when thou fallest, there shall be none to deliver thee."

10. "But, however, in other places," continue the objectors, "Solomon does assert plainly, 'There is no man that sinneth not;' (1 Kings viii. 46; 2 Chron. vi. 36;) yea, "There is not a just man upon earth that doeth good, and sinneth not.' (Eccles. vii. 20.)" I answer, Without doubt, thus it was in the days of Solomon. Yea, thus it was from Adam to Moses, from Moses to Solomon, and from Solomon to Christ. There was then no man that sinned not. Even from the day that sin entered into the world, there was not a just man upon earth that did good and sinned not, until the Son of God was manifested to take away our sins. It is unquestionably true, that "the heir, as long as he is a child, differeth nothing from a servant." And that even so they (all the holy men of old, who were under the Jewish dispensation) were,

during that infant state of the Church, "in bondage under the elements of the world." "But when the fulness of the time was come, God sent forth his Son, made under the law, to redeem them that were under the law, that they might receive the adoption of sons;"—that they might receive that "grace which is now made manifest by the appearing of our Saviour, Jesus Christ, who hath abolished death, and brought life and immortality to light through the gospel." (2 Tim. i. 10.) Now, therefore, they "are no more servants, but sons." So that, whatsoever was the case of those under the law, we may safely affirm with St. John, that, since the gospel was given, "he that is born of God sinneth not."

11. It is of great importance to observe, and that more carefully than is commonly done, the wide difference there is between the Jewish and the Christian dispensation; and that ground of it which the same Apostle assigns in the seventh chapter of his Gospel. (verses 38, &c.) After he had there related, those words of our blessed Lord, "He that believeth on me, as the Scripture hath said, out of his belly shall flow rivers of living water," he immediately subjoins, "This spake he of the Spirit," ὃ ἔμελλον λαμβάνειν οἱ πιστεύοντες εἰς αὐτόν, – *which they who should believe on him were afterwards to receive.* For the Holy Ghost was not yet given, because that Jesus was not yet glorified." Now, the Apostle cannot mean here, (as some have taught,) that the mir-

acle-working power of the Holy Ghost was
not yet given. For this was given; our Lord
had given it to all the Apostles, when he first
sent them forth to preach the gospel. He
then gave them power over unclean spirits
to cast them out; power to heal the sick; yea,
to raise the dead. But the Holy Ghost was
not yet given in his sanctifying graces, as he
was after Jesus was glorified. It was then
when "he ascended up on high, and led captivity captive," that he "received" those
"gifts for men, yea, even for the rebellious,
that the Lord God might dwell among
them." And when the day of Pentecost was
fully come, then first it was, that they who
"waited for the promise of the Father" were
made more than conquerors over sin by the
Holy Ghost given unto them.

12. That this great salvation from sin was
not given till Jesus was glorified, St. Peter
also plainly testifies; where, speaking of his
brethren in the flesh, as now "receiving the
end of their faith, the salvation of their
souls," he adds, (1 Peter i. 9, 10, &c.,) "Of
which salvation the Prophets have inquired
and searched diligently, who prophesied of
the grace" that is, the gracious dispensation,
"that should come unto you: Searching
what, or what manner of time the Spirit of
Christ which was in them did signify, when
it testified beforehand the sufferings of
Christ. and the glory," the glorious salvation, "that should follow. Unto whom it was
revealed, that not unto themselves, but unto
us they did minister the things which are

now reported unto you by them that have
preached the Gospel unto you with the Holy
Ghost sent down from heaven;" viz., at the
day of Pentecost, and so unto all generations, into the hearts of all true believers.
On this ground, even "the grace which was
brought unto them by the revelation of Jesus Christ," the Apostle might well build
that strong exhortation, "Wherefore girding
up the loins of your mind,—as he which
hath called you is holy, so be ye holy in all
manner of conversation."

13. Those who have duly considered these
things must allow, that the privileges of
Christians are in no wise to be measured by
what the Old Testament records concerning
those who were under the Jewish dispensation; seeing the fulness of times is now
come; the Holy Ghost is now given; the
great salvation of God is brought unto men,
by the revelation of Jesus Christ. The kingdom of heaven is now set up on earth; concerning which the Spirit of God declared of
old, (so far is David from being the pattern
or standard of Christian perfection,) "He
that is feeble among them at that day, shall
be as David; and the house of David shall be
as God, as the angel of the Lord before
them." (Zech. xii. 8.)

14. If, therefore, you would prove that the
Apostle's words, "He that is born of God
sinneth not," are not to be understood according to their plain, natural, obvious
meaning, it is from the New Testament you

are to bring your proofs, else you will fight
as one that beateth the air. And the first of
these which is usually brought is taken from
the examples recorded in the New Testament. "The Apostles themselves," it is said,
"committed sin; nay, the greatest of them,
Peter and Paul: St. Paul, by his sharp contention with Barnabas; and St. Peter, by his
dissimulation at Antioch." Well: Suppose
both Peter and Paul did then commit sin;
what is it you would infer from hence? That
all the other Apostles committed sin sometimes? There is no shadow of proof in this.
Or would you thence infer, that all the other
Christians of the apostolic age committed
sin? Worse and worse: This is such an inference as, one would imagine, a man in his
senses could never have thought of. Or will
you argue thus: "If two of the Apostles did
once commit sin, then all other Christians,
in all ages, do and will commit sin as long as
they live?" Alas, my brother! a child of common understanding would be ashamed of
such reasoning as this. Least of all can you
with any colour of argument infer, that any
man must commit sin at all. No: God forbid
we should thus speak! No necessity of sinning was laid upon them. The grace of God
was surely sufficient for them. And it is sufficient for us at this day. With the temptation which fell on them, there was a way to
escape; as there is to every soul of man in
every temptation. So that whosoever is
tempted to any sin, need not yield; for no
man is tempted above that he is able to

bear.

15. "But St. Paul besought the Lord thrice, and yet he could not escape from his temptation." Let us consider his own words literally translated: "There was given to me a thorn to the flesh, an angel" (or messenger) "of Satan, to buffet me. Touching this, I besought the Lord thrice, that it" (or he) "might depart from me. And he said unto me, My grace is sufficient for thee: For my strength is made perfect in weakness. Most gladly, therefore, will I rather glory in" these "my weaknesses, that the strength of Christ may rest upon me. Therefore I take pleasure in weaknesses;—for when I am weak, then am I strong."

16. As this scripture is one of the strongholds of the patrons of sin, it may be proper to weigh it thoroughly. Let it be observed then, First, it does by no means appear that this thorn, whatsoever it was, occasioned St. Paul to commit sin; much less laid him under any necessity of doing so. Therefore, from hence it can never be proved that any Christian must commit sin. Secondly, the ancient Fathers inform us, it was bodily pain: "a violent headache, saith Tertullian; (*De Pudic.*;) to which both Chrysostom and St. Jerome agree. St. Cyprian* expresses it, a little more generally, in those terms: "Many and grievous torments of the flesh and of the body."† Thirdly, to this exactly agree the Apostle's own words, "A thorn to the flesh

---

*De Mortalitate

to smite, beat, or buffet me." "My strength is made perfect in weakness:"—Which same word occurs no less than four times in these two verses only. But, Fourthly, whatsoever it was, it could not be either inward or outward sin. It could no more be inward stirrings, than outward expressions, of pride, anger, or lust. This is manifest, beyond all possible exception, from the words that immediately follow: "Most gladly will I glory in" these "my weaknesses, that the strength of Christ may rest upon me." What! did he glory in pride, in anger, in lust? Was it through these *weaknesses*, that the strength of Christ rested upon him? He goes on: "Therefore I take pleasure in weaknesses; for when I am weak, then am I strong;" that is, when I am weak *in body*, then am I strong *in spirit*. But will any man dare to say, "When I am weak by pride or lust, then am I strong in spirit?" I call you all to record this day, who find the strength of Christ resting upon you, can you glory in anger, or pride, or lust? Can you take pleasure in these infirmities? Do these weaknesses make you strong? Would you not leap into hell, were it possible, to escape them? Even by yourselves, then, judge, whether the Apostle could glory and take pleasure in them! Let it be, Lastly, observed, that this thorn was given to St. Paul above fourteen years before he wrote this Epistle; which itself was wrote several years before he fin-

---

†*Carnis et corporis multa ac gravia tormenta.*

ished his course. So that he had after this, a long course to run, many battles to fight, many victories to gain, and great increase to receive in all the gifts of God, and the knowledge of Jesus Christ. Therefore from any spiritual weakness (if such it had been) which he at that time felt, we could by no means infer that he was never made strong; that Paul the aged, the father in Christ, still laboured under the same weaknesses; that he was in no higher state till the day of his death. From all which it appears that this instance of St. Paul is quite foreign to the question, and does in nowise clash with the assertion of St. John, "He that is born of God sinneth not."

17. "But does not St. James directly contradict this? His words are, 'In many things we offend all,' (Jas. iii. 2:) And is not offending the same as committing sin?" In this place, I allow it is: I allow the persons here spoken of did commit sin; yea, that they all committed many sins. But who are the persons here spoken of? Why, those many masters or teachers whom God had not sent; (probably the same vain men who taught that faith without works, which is so sharply reproved in the preceding chapter;) not the Apostle himself, nor any real Christian. That in the word we (used by a figure of speech common in all other, as well as the inspired, writings) the Apostle could not possibly include himself or any other true believer, appears evidently, First, from the same word in the ninth verse:—"Therewith," saith he,

"bless we God and therewith curse we men. Out of the same mouth proceedeth blessing and cursing." True; but not out of the mouth of the Apostle, nor of anyone who is in Christ a new creature. Secondly, from the verse immediately preceding the text, and manifestly connected with it: "My brethren, be not many masters," (or teachers,) "knowing that we shall receive the greater condemnation." "For in many things *we* offend all." *We!* Who? Not the Apostles, not true believers; but they who know they should *receive the greater condemnation*, because of those many offences. But this could not be spoke of the Apostle himself, or of any who trod in his steps, seeing "there is no condemnation to them who walk not after the flesh, but after the Spirit." Nay, Thirdly, the very verse itself proves, that "we offend all," cannot be spoken either of all men, or of all Christians: For in it there immediately follows the mention of a man who *offends not*, as the *we* first mentioned did; from whom, therefore, he is professedly contradistinguished, and pronounced *a perfect man*.

18. So clearly does St. James explain himself, and fix the meaning of his own words. Yet, lest any one should still remain in doubt, St. John, writing many years after St. James, puts the matter entirely out of dispute, by the express declarations above recited. But here a fresh difficulty may arise: How shall we reconcile St. John with himself? In one place he declares, "Whosoever

is born of God doth not commit sin;" and
again,—"We know that he which is born of
God sinneth not:" And yet in another he
saith, "If we say that we have no sin, we deceive ourselves, and the truth is not in us;"
and again,—"If we say that we have not
sinned, we make him a liar, and his word is
not in us."

19. As great a difficulty as this may at first
appear, it vanishes away, if we observe,
First, that the tenth verse fixes the sense of
the eighth: "If we say we have no sin," in the
former, being explained by, "If we say we
have not sinned," in the latter verse.
Secondly, that the point under present consideration is not whether we *have or have
not sinned heretofore*; and neither of these
verses asserts that we *do sin, or commit sin
now*. Thirdly, that the ninth verse explains
both the eighth and tenth. "If we confess
our sins, he is faithful and just to forgive us
our sins, and to cleanse us from all unrighteousness:" As if he had said, "I have before
affirmed, `The blood of Jesus Christ
cleanseth us from all sin; but let no man
say, I need it not; I have no sin to be
cleansed from. If we say that we have no sin,
that we have not sinned, we deceive
ourselves, and make God a liar: But if we
confess our sins, he is faithful and just,' not
only 'to forgive our sins,' but also 'to cleanse
us from all unrighteousness:' that we may
'go and sin no more.'"

20. St. John, therefore, is well consistent with himself, as well as with the other holy writers; as will yet more evidently appear, if we place all his assertions touching this matter in one view: He declares, First, the blood of Jesus Christ cleanseth us from all sin. Secondly, no man can say, I have not sinned, I have no sin to be cleansed from. Thirdly, but God is ready both to forgive our past sins and to save us from them for the time to come. Fourthly, "These things I write unto you," saith the Apostle, "that ye may not sin. But if any man" should "sin," *or have sinned*, (as the word might be rendered,) he need not continue in sin; seeing "we have an Advocate with the Father, Jesus Christ the righteous." Thus far all is clear. But lest any doubt should remain in a point of so vast importance, the Apostle resumes this subject in the third chapter, and largely explains his own meaning. "Little children," saith he, "let no man deceive you:" (As though I had given any encouragement to those that continue in sin:) "He that doeth righteousness is righteous, even as He is righteous. He that committeth sin is of the devil; for the devil sinneth from the beginning. For this purpose the Son of God was manifested, that he might destroy the works of the devil. Whosoever is born of God doth not commit sin: For his seed remaineth in him; and he cannot sin, because he is born of God. In this the children of God are manifest, and the children of the devil." (Verses 7-10.) Here the point, which

till then might possibly have admitted of some doubt in weak minds, is purposely settled by the last of the inspired writers, and decided in the clearest manner. In conformity, therefore, both to the doctrine of St. John, and to the whole tenor of the New Testament, we fix this conclusion—*A Christian is so far perfect, as not to commit sin.*

21. This is the glorious privilege of every Christian; yea, though he be but *a babe in Christ.* But it is only of those who *are strong* in the Lord, "and "have overcome the wicked one," or rather of those who "have known him that is from the beginning," that it can be affirmed they are in such a sense perfect, as, Secondly, to be freed from evil thoughts and evil tempers. First, from evil or sinful thoughts. But here let it be observed, that thoughts concerning evil are not always evil thoughts; that a thought concerning sin, and a sinful thought, are widely different. A man, for instance, may think of a murder which another has committed; and yet this is no evil or sinful thought. So our blessed Lord himself doubtless thought of, or understood the thing spoken by the devil, when he said, "All these things will I give thee, if thou wilt fall down and worship me." Yet had he no evil or sinful thought; nor indeed was capable of having any. And even hence it follows, that neither have real Christians: for "every one that is perfect is as his Master." (Luke vi. 40) Therefore, if He was free from evil or sinful thoughts, so are they likewise.

They may expect to be made free from sinful thoughts

22. And, indeed, whence should evil thoughts proceed, in the servant who is *as his Master*? "Out of the heart of man" (if at all) "proceed evil thoughts." (Mark vii. 21) If, therefore, his heart be no longer evil, then evil thoughts can no longer proceed out of it. If the tree were corrupt, so would be the fruit: But the tree is good; the fruit, therefore is good also; (Matt. xii. 33) our Lord himself bearing witness, "Every good tree bringeth forth good fruit. A good tree cannot bring forth evil fruit," as "a corrupt tree cannot bring forth good fruit." (Matt vii. 17, 18)

23. The same happy privilege of real Christians, St. Paul asserts from his own experience. "The weapons of our warfare," saith he, "are not carnal, but mighty through God to the pulling down of strong-holds; casting down imaginations" (or *reasonings* rather, for so the word λογιμοὺς signifies; all the reasonings of pride and unbelief against the declarations, promises, or gifts of God) "and every high thing that exalteth itself against the knowledge of God, and bringing into captivity every thought to the obedience of Christ." (2 Cor. x. 4, &c.)

24. And as Christians indeed are freed from evil thoughts, so are they, Secondly, from evil tempers. This is evident from the above-mentioned declaration of our Lord himself: "The disciple is not above his Master; but every one that is perfect shall be as his Master." He had been delivering, just

They may expect to be made free from sinful tempers

before, some of the sublimest doctrines of Christianity, and some of the most grievous to flesh and blood. "I say unto you, love your enemies, do good to them which hate you;—and unto him that smiteth thee on the one cheek, offer also the other." Now these he well knew the world would not receive; and, therefore, immediately adds, "Can the blind lead the blind? Will they not both fall into the ditch?" As if he had said, "Do not confer with flesh and blood touching these things,—with men void of spiritual discernment, the eyes of whose understanding God hath not opened,—lest they and you perish together." In the next verse he removes the two grand objections with which these wise fools meet us at every turn: "These things are too grievous to be borne," or, "They are too high to be attained," saying, "'The disciple is not above his Master;' therefore, if I have suffered, be content to tread in my steps. And doubt ye not then, but I will fulfil my word: 'For every one that is perfect shall be as his Master.'" But his Master was free from all sinful tempers. So, therefore, is his disciple, even every real Christian.

25. Every one of these can say, with St. Paul, "I am crucified with Christ: Nevertheless I live; yet not I, but Christ liveth in me:"— Words that manifestly describe a deliverance from inward as well as from outward sin. This is expressed both negatively, *I live not*; (my evil nature, the body of sin, is destroyed;) and positively, *Christ liveth in me*; and, therefore, all that is holy, and just, and

good. Indeed, both these, *Christ liveth in me*, and *I live not*, are inseparably connected; for "what communion hath light with darkness, or Christ with Belial?"

26. He, therefore, who liveth in true believers, hath "purified their hearts by faith;" insomuch that every one that hath Christ in him the hope of glory, purifieth himself, even as he is pure" (1 John iii. 3.) He is purified from pride; for Christ was lowly of heart. He is pure from self-will or desire; for Christ desired only to do the will of his Father, and to finish his work. And he is pure from anger, in the common sense of the word; for Christ was meek and gentle, patient and long-suffering. I say, in the common sense of the word; for all anger is not evil. We read of our Lord himself, (Mark iii. 5,) that he once "looked round with anger." But with what kind of anger? The next word shows, συλλυπούμενος, being, at the same time "grieved for the hardness of their hearts." So then he was angry at the sin, and in the same moment grieved for the sinners; angry or displeased at the offence, but sorry for the offenders. With anger, yea, hatred, he looked upon the thing; with grief and love upon the persons. Go, thou that art perfect, and do likewise. Be thus angry, and thou sinnest not; feeling a displacency at every offence against God, but only love and tender compassion to the offender.

27. Thus doth Jesus "save his people from their sins:" And not only from outward sins,

but also from the sins of their hearts; from
evil thoughts and from evil tempers.
—"True," say some, "we shall thus be saved
from our sins; but not till death; not in this
world." But how are we to reconcile this
with the express words of St. John?
—"Herein is our love made perfect, that we
may have boldness in the day of judgement.
Because as he is, so are we in this world."
The Apostle here, beyond all contradiction,
speaks of himself and other living Christians, of whom (as though he had foreseen
this very evasion, and set himself to over-
turn it from the foundation) he flatly af-
firms, that not only at or after death but *in
this world* they are as their Master. (1 John
iv. 17.)

28. Exactly agreeable to this are his words
in the first chapter of this Epistle, (verse 5,
&c.,) "God is light, and in him is no darkness at all. If we walk in the light,—we have
fellowship one with another, and the blood
of Jesus Christ his Son cleanseth us from all
sin." And again, "If we confess our sins, he
is faithful and just to forgive us our sins,
and to cleanse us from all unrighteousness."
Now it is evident, the Apostle here also
speaks of a deliverance wrought *in this
world.* For he saith not, the blood of Christ
will cleanse at the hour of death, or in the
day of judgment, but, it "cleanseth," at the
time present, "us," living Christians, "from
all sin." And it is equally evident, that if *any
sin* remain, we are not cleansed from *all sin*:
If any unrighteousness remain in the soul, it

is not cleansed from all unrighteousness. Neither let any sinner against his own soul say, that this relates to justification only, or the cleansing us from the guilt of sin. First, because this is confounding together what the Apostle clearly distinguishes, who mentions first, *to forgive us our sins*, and then *to cleanse us from all unrighteousness.* "Secondly, because this is asserting justification by works, in the strongest sense possible; it is making all inward as well as outward holiness necessarily previous to justification. For if the cleansing here spoken of is no other than the cleansing us from the guilt of sin, then we are not cleansed from guilt; that is, are not justified, unless on condition of "walking in the light, as he is in the light." It remains, then, that Christians are saved in this world from all sin, from all unrighteousness; that they are now in such a sense perfect, as not to commit sin, and to be freed from evil thoughts and evil tempers."

29. Thus hath the Lord fulfilled the things he spake by his holy prophets, which have been since the world began;—by Moses in particular, saying, (Deut. xxx. 6.) I "will circumcise thine heart, and the heart of thy seed, to love the Lord thy God with all thy heart, and with all thy soul;" by David, crying out, "Create in me a clean heart, and renew a right spirit within me;"—and most remarkably by Ezekiel, in those words: "Then will I sprinkle clean water upon you, and ye shall be clean; From all your filthiness, and

from all your idols, will I cleanse you. A new heart also will I give you, and a new spirit will I put within you;—and cause you to walk in my statutes, and ye shall keep my judgements, and do them.—Ye shall be my people, and I will be your God. I will also save you from all your uncleannesses.—Thus saith the Lord your God, In the day that I shall have cleansed you from all your iniquities,—the Heathen shall know that I the Lord build the ruined places;—I the Lord have spoken it, and I will do it." (Ezek. xxxvi. 25, &c.)

30. "Having therefore these promises, dearly beloved," both in the Law and in the Prophets, and having the prophetic word confirmed unto us in the Gospel, by our blessed Lord and his Apostles; "let us cleanse ourselves from all filthiness of flesh and spirit, perfecting holiness in the fear of God." "Let us fear, lest" so many "promises being made us of entering into his rest," which he that hath entered into, has ceased from his own works, "any of us should come short of it." "This one thing let us do, forgetting those things which are behind, and reaching forth unto those things which are before, let us press toward the mark, for the prize of the high calling of God in Christ Jesus;" crying unto him day and night, till we also are "delivered from the bondage of corruption, into the glorious liberty of the sons of God!"

CHARLES WESLEY,
POEM "WRESTLING JACOB" (1742)

Comment: The following poem is considered by many to be Charles Wesley's poetic masterpiece. When John Wesley spoke about his brother at the Methodist Conference in 1788, immediately after Charles's death, he stated that "Dr. [Isaac] Watts did not scruple to say 'that single poem, Wrestling Jacob, was worth all the verses he himself had written.'" Charles Wesley takes the story of Jacob wrestling the mysterious stranger (Genesis 32:24-32) as a metaphor for the soul's wresting with God. The drama in the poem lies in its withheld secret: what is the mysterious name of the stranger, the secret name of God? The question is repeated over and over at the end of verses until at last "The morning breaks, the shadows flee," and the name is revealed. I'm certainly not telling: you'll have to read the poem to find out what it is. A distinctive feature of the formatting of the poem in the original publication is that Charles Wesley utilized small capitals for "LOVE" and "UNIVERSAL LOVE" as ways of naming God. This recalls the manner in which the divine name had been given in English-translations of the Old Testament, where "LORD," as a circumlocution for the divine name, was placed in small capitals. Since I think this formatting is significant, I have restored it in this text, although it does not appear in the Osborn edition of the *Poetical Works*.

Source: The poem was originally published in *Hymns and Sacred Poems* (1742, pp. 115-118). The version given here is from Osborn, *Poetical Works*, 2:173-176.

Wrestling Jacob

Come, O Thou Traveller unknown,
Whom still I hold, but cannot see,
My company before is gone,
And I am left alone with Thee;
With Thee all night I mean to stay,
And wrestle till the break of day.

I need not tell Thee who I am,
My misery or sin declare,
Thyself hast call'd me by my name,
Look on Thy hands, and read it there;
But who, I ask Thee, who art Thou?
Tell me Thy name, and tell me now.

In vain Thou strugglest to get free,
I never will unloose my hold;
Art thou the Man that died for me?
The secret of Thy love unfold;
Wrestling I will not let Thee go
Till I Thy name, Thy nature know.

Wilt Thou not yet to me reveal
Thy new, unutterable name?
Tell me, I still beseech Thee, tell;
To know it now resolved I am;
Wrestling I will not let Thee go
Till I Thy name, Thy nature know.

'Tis all in vain to hold Thy tongue,
Or touch the hollow of my thigh;
Though every sinew be unstrung,
Out of my arms Thou shalt not fly;
Wrestling I will not let Thee go
Till I Thy name, Thy nature know.

What though my shrinking flesh complain,
And murmur to contend so long,
I rise superior to my pain,
When I am weak then I am strong;
And when my all of strength shall fail,
I shall with the God-man prevail.

My strength is gone, my nature dies,
I sink beneath Thy weighty hand,
Faint to revive, and fall to rise;
I fall, and yet by faith I stand,
I stand, and will not let Thee go,
Till I Thy name, Thy nature know.

Yield to me now; for I am weak,
But confident in self-despair:
Speak to my heart, in blessings speak,
Be conquer'd by my instant prayer;
Speak, or Thou never hence shalt move,
And tell me if Thy name is LOVE.

'Tis Love! 'tis Love! Thou diedst for me;
I hear Thy whisper in my heart:
The morning breaks, the shadows flee:
Pure UNIVERSAL LOVE Thou art;
To me, to all Thy bowels move;
Thy nature, and Thy name is LOVE.

My prayer hath power with God; the grace
Unspeakable I now receive,
Through faith I see Thee face to face;
I see Thee face to face, and live:
In vain I have not wept and strove;
Thy nature, and Thy name is Love.

I know Thee, Saviour, who Thou art,
Jesus, the feeble sinner's Friend;
Nor wilt Thou with the night depart,
But stay, and love me to the end;
Thy mercies never shall remove;
Thy nature, and Thy name is Love.

The Sun of Righteousness on me
Hath rose with healing in His wings;
Wither'd my nature's strength, from Thee
My soul its life and succour brings;
My help is all laid up above;
Thy nature, and Thy name is Love.

Contented now upon my thigh
I halt, till life's short journey end;
All helplessness, all weakness, I
On Thee alone for strength depend,
Nor have I power from Thee to move;
Thy nature, and Thy name is Love.

Lame as I am, I take the prey,
Hell, earth, and sin with ease o'ercome;
I leap for joy, pursue my way,
And as a bounding hart fly home,
Through all eternity to prove,
Thy nature, and Thy name is Love.

Item 8:

John and Charles Wesley, "The Nature, Design, and General Rules of the United Societies in London, Bristol, Kingswood, Newcastle-upon-Tyne, &c." (1743)

Comment: The following rules functioned as a basic contract for persons in early Methodist societies, laying out the terms for entry into the societies and the terms for continuing in them. David Lowes Watson has shown that the basic, weekly work of each class (the smaller groups into which societies were divided) was to ask whether each member had kept each of the rules every week. These rules remain in effect in Methodist churches throughout the world, and up until the beginning of the twentieth century (in the US) persons could not be enrolled as members of Methodist societies or congregations (as societies came to be called) unless they had demonstrated their sincerity in keeping these rules through a period of probationary membership in the local society that would last from a few months to a few years. Although the document is signed by John and Charles Wesley, it is written in the first-person singular, and one suspects that John Wesley was the author of these rules.

Source: Jackson, *Works*, 8:269-271.

1. In the latter end of the year 1739, eight or ten persons came to me in London, who appeared to be deeply convinced of sin, and earnestly groaning for redemption. They desired (as did two or three more the next

day) that I would spend some time with
them in prayer, and advise them how to flee
from the wrath to come; which they saw
continually hanging over their heads. That
we might have more time for this great
work, I appointed a day when they might all
come together, which from thenceforward
they did every week, namely, on Thursday,
in the evening. To these, and as many more
as desired to join with them, (for their number increased daily,) I gave those advices,
from time to time, which I judged most
needful for them; and we always concluded
our meeting with prayer suited to their several necessities.

2. This was the rise of the United Society,
first in London, and then in other places.
Such a society is no other than "a company
of men having the form and seeking the
power of godliness, united in order to pray
together, to receive the word of exhortation,
and to watch over one another in love, that
they may help each other to work out their
salvation."

3. That it may the more easily be discerned,
whether they are indeed working out their
own salvation, each society is divided into
smaller companies, called *classes*, according
to their respective places of abode. There
are about twelve persons in every class; one
of whom is styled *the Leader*. It is his business, (1.) To see each person in his class
once a week at least, in order to inquire how
their souls prosper; to advise, reprove, com-

fort, or exhort, as occasion may require; to receive what they are willing to give toward the relief of the poor. (2.) To meet the Minister and the Stewards of the society once a week; in order to inform the Minister of any that are sick, or of any that walk disorderly, and will not be reproved; to pay to the Stewards what they have received of their several classes in the week preceding; and to show their account of what each person has contributed.

4. There is one only condition previously required in those who desire admission into these societies,—a desire "to flee from the wrath to come, to be saved from their sins:" But, wherever this is really fixed in the soul, it will be shown by its fruits. It is therefore expected of all who continue therein, that they should continue to evidence their desire of salvation,

The prerequisite for membership

First, by doing no harm, by avoiding evil in every kind; especially that which is most generally practised: Such is, the taking the name of God in vain; the profaning the day of the Lord, either by doing ordinary work thereon, or by buying or selling; drunkenness, buying or selling spirituous liquors, or drinking them, unless in cases of extreme necessity; fighting, quarrelling, brawling; brother going to law with brother; returning evil for evil, or railing for railing; the using many words in buying or selling; the buying or selling unaccustomed goods; the giving or taking things on usury,that is, unlawful

Conditions for continued membership: 1. avoiding evil

interest; uncharitable or unprofitable conversation, particularly speaking evil of Ma-
gistrates or of Ministers; doing to others as
we would not they should do unto us; doing
what we know is not for the glory of God, as
the "putting on of gold or costly apparel;"
the taking such diversions as cannot be used
in the name of the Lord Jesus; the singing
those songs, or reading those books, which
do not tend to the knowledge or love of
God; softness, and needless self-indulgence;
laying up treasures upon earth; borrowing
without a probability of paying; or taking up
goods without a probability of paying for
them.

5. It is expected of all who continue in these
societies, that they should continue to evidence their desire of salvation,

Secondly, by doing good, by being, in every
kind, merciful after their power; as they
have opportunity, doing good of every possible sort, and as far as is possible, to all
men;—to their bodies, of the ability which
God giveth, by giving food to the hungry, by
clothing the naked, by visiting or helping
them that are sick, or in prison;—to their
souls, by instructing reproving, or exhorting
all they have any intercourse with; tramp-
ling under foot that enthusiastic doctrine of
devils, that "we are not to do good unless
our heart be free to it:" By doing good especially to them that are of the household of
faith, or groaning so to be; employing them
preferably to others, buying one of another;

Conditions for continued membership: 2. doing good

helping each other in business; and so much the more, because the world will love its own, and them only: By all possible diligence and frugality, that the gospel be not blamed: By running with patience the race that is set before them, "denying themselves, and taking up their cross daily;" submitting to bear the reproach of Christ, to be as the filth and off-scouring of the world; and looking that men should "say all manner of evil of them falsely for the Lord's sake."

6. It is expected of all who desire to continue in these societies, that they should continue to evidence their desire of salvation,

Thirdly, by attending upon all the ordinances of God. Such are, the public worship of God; the ministry of the word, either read or expounded; the supper of the Lord; family and private prayer; searching the Scriptures; and fasting, or abstinence.

Conditions for continued membership: 3. attending upon the ordinances

7. These are the General Rules of our societies; all which we are taught of God to observe, even in his written word, the only rule, and the sufficient rule, both of our faith and practice. And all these, we know, his Spirit writes on every truly awakened heart. If there be any among us who observe them not, who habitually break any of them, let it be made known unto them who watch over that soul as they that must give an account. We will admonish him of the error of his ways; we will bear with him for a season: But then if he repent not, he hath no more

place among us. We have delivered our own souls.

JOHN WESLEY,
CHARLES WESLEY.

May 1, 1743.

JOHN WESLEY, SERMON ON "THE MEANS OF GRACE" (1745)

Comment: John Wesley wrote the following sermon in response to the teachings of an eccentric group of London Moravians who maintained that if one had not experienced the assurance of pardon, one should "be still, and wait upon the LORD." A further implication they drew from this teaching was that those who had not yet experienced assurance (and whom they presumed to be unconverted) should not use any of the means of grace. Wesley strongly objected, and the sermon shows his consistent view that one should "wait upon the LORD" in all the means that God had intended.

Source: Jackson, *Works*, 5:185-201.

"Ye are gone away from mine ordinances, and have not kept them." Malachi iii. 7.

I. 1. BUT are there any *ordinances* now, since life and immortality were brought to light by the gospel? Are there, under the Christian dispensation, any *means ordained* of God, as the usual channels of his grace? This question could never have been proposed in the apostolical church, unless by one who openly avowed himself to be a Heathen; the whole body of Christians being agreed, that Christ had ordained certain outward means, for conveying his grace into the souls of men. Their constant practice set

I. The occasion of the sermon: neglect or abuse of the means of grace

this beyond all dispute; for so long as "all that believed were together, and had all things common," (Acts ii. 44,) "they continued steadfastly in the teaching of the Apostles, and in breaking of bread, and in prayers." (Verse 42.)

2. But in process of time, when "the love of many waxed cold," some began to mistake the *means* for the *end*, and to place religion rather in doing those outward works, than in a heart renewed after the image of God. They forgot that "the end of" every "commandment is love, out of a pure heart," with "faith unfeigned;" the loving the Lord their God with all their heart, and their neighbour as themselves; and the being purified from pride, anger, and evil desire, by a "faith of the operation of God." Others seemed to imagine, that though religion did not principally consist in these outward means, yet there was something in them wherewith God was well pleased; something that would still make them acceptable in his sight, though they were not exact in the weightier matters of the law, in justice, mercy, and the love of God.

Abuse of the means of grace

3. It is evident, in those who abused them thus, they did not conduce to the end for which they were ordained: Rather, the things which should have been for their health, were to them an occasion of falling. They were so far from receiving any blessing therein, that they only drew down a curse upon their head; so far from growing more

heavenly in heart and life, that they were
two-fold more the children of hell than before. Others, clearly perceiving that these
means did not convey the grace of God to
those children of the devil, began, from this
particular case, to draw a general conclusion,—that they were not means of conveying the grace of God.

4. Yet the number of those who *abused* the
ordinances of God, was far greater than of
those who *despised* them, till certain men
arose, not only of great understanding,
(sometimes joined with considerable learn-
ing,) but who likewise appeared to be men
of love, experimentally acquainted with
true, inward religion. Some of these were
burning and shining lights, persons famous
in their generations, and such as had well
deserved of the church of Christ, for stand-
ing in the gap against the overflowings of
ungodliness.

It cannot be supposed, that these holy and
venerable men intended any more, at first,
than to show that outward religion is nothing worth, without the religion of the heart;
that "God is a Spirit, and they who worship
him must worship him in spirit and in
truth;" that, therefore, external worship is
lost labor, without a heart devoted to God;
that the outward ordinances of God then
profit much, when they advance inward
holiness, but, when they advance it not, are
unprofitable and void, are lighter than vanity; yea, that when they are used, as it were

in the place of this, they are an utter abomination to the Lord.

5. Yet it is not strange, if some of these, being strongly convinced of that horrid profanation of the ordinances of God, which had spread itself over the whole church, and well nigh driven true religion out of the world,—in their fervent zeal for the glory of God, and the recovery of souls from that fatal delusion,—spake as if outward religion were absolutely nothing, as if it had no place in the religion of Christ. It is not surprising at all, if they should not always have expressed themselves with sufficient caution; so that unwary hearers might believe they condemned all outward means, as altogether unprofitable, and as not designed of God to be the ordinary channels of conveying his grace into the souls of men.

Nay, it is not impossible, some of these holy men did, at length, themselves fall into this opinion; in particular those who, not by choice, but by the providence of God, were cut off from all these ordinances; perhaps wandering up and down, having no certain abiding-place, or dwelling in dens and caves of the earth. These, experiencing the grace of God in themselves, though they were deprived of all outward means, might infer that the same grace would be given to them who of set purpose abstained from them.

6. And experience shows how easily this notion spreads, and insinuates itself into the minds of men; especially of those who are

Neglect of the means of grace

thoroughly awakened out of the sleep of death, and begin to feel the weight of their sins a burden too heavy to be borne. These are usually impatient of their present state; and, trying every way to escape from it, they are always ready to catch at any new thing, any new proposal of ease or happiness. They have probably tried most outward means, and found no ease in them; it may be, more and more of remorse, and fear, and sorrow, and condemnation. It is easy, therefore, to persuade these, that it is better for them to abstain from all those means. They are already weary of striving (as it seems) in vain, of labouring in the fire; and are therefore glad of any pretence to cast aside that wherein their soul has no pleasure, to give over the painful strife, and sink down into an indolent inactivity.

II. 1. In the following discourse, I propose to examine at large, whether there are any means of grace.

II. Basic principles about the means of grace

By "means of grace" I understand outward signs, words, or actions, ordained of God, and appointed for this end, to be the ordinary channels whereby he might convey to men, preventing, justifying, or sanctifying grace.

Definition of means of grace

I use this expression, means of grace, because I know none better; and because it has been generally used in the Christian Church for many ages,—in particular by our own Church, which directs us to bless God both for the means of grace, and hope of glory; and teaches us, that a sacrament is "an outward sign of inward grace, and a means whereby we receive the same."

The chief of these means are prayer, whether in secret or with the great congregation; searching the Scriptures; (which implies reading, hearing, and meditating thereon;) and receiving the Lord's supper, eating bread and drinking wine in remembrance of Him: And these we believe to be ordained of God, as the ordinary channels of conveying his grace to the souls of men.

2. But we allow, that the whole value of the means depends on their actual subservience to the end of religion; that, consequently, all these means, when separate from the end, are less than nothing and vanity; that if they do not actually conduce to the knowledge and love of God, they are not acceptable in his sight; yea, rather, they are an abomination before him, a stink in his nostrils; he is weary to bear them. Above all, if they are used as a kind of *commutation* for the religion they were designed to subserve, it is not easy to find words for the enormous folly and wickedness of thus turning God's arms against himself; of keeping Christianity out of the heart by those very means which were ordained for the bringing it in.

The means of grace and the end of religion

3. We allow, likewise, that all outward means whatever, if separate from the Spirit of God, cannot profit at all, cannot conduce, in any degree, either to the knowledge or love of God. Without controversy, the help

that is done upon earth, He doeth it himself. It is He alone who, by his own almighty power, worketh in us what is pleasing in his sight; and all outward things, unless He work in them and by them, are mere weak and beggarly elements. Whosoever, therefore, imagines there is any intrinsic power in any means whatsoever, does greatly err, not knowing the Scriptures, neither the power of God. We know that there is no inherent power in the words that are spoken in prayer, in the letter of Scripture read, the sound thereof heard, or the bread and wine received in the Lord's supper; but that it is God alone who is the Giver of every good gift, the Author of all grace; that the whole power is of Him, whereby, through any of these, there is any blessing conveyed to our souls. We know, likewise, that he is able to give the same grace, though there were no means on the face of the earth. In this sense, we may affirm, that, with regard to God, there is no such thing as means; seeing he is equally able to work whatsoever pleaseth him, by any, or by none at all.

4. We allow farther, that the use of all means whatever will never atone for one sin; that it is the blood of Christ alone, whereby any sinner can be reconciled to God; there being no other propitiation for our sins, no other fountain for sin and uncleanness. Every believer in Christ is deeply convinced that there is no merit but in Him; that there is no merit in any of his own works; not in uttering the prayer, or search-

ing the Scripture, or hearing the word of God, or eating of that bread and drinking of that cup. So that if no more be intended by the expression some have used, "Christ is the only means of grace," than this,—that He is the only meritorious cause of it, it cannot be gainsayed by any who know the grace of God.

5. Yet once more: We allow, though it is a melancholy truth, that a large proportion of those who are called Christians, do to this day abuse the means of grace to the destruction of their souls. This is doubtless the case with all those who rest content in the form of godliness, without the power. Either they fondly presume they are Christians already, because they do thus and thus,—although Christ was never yet revealed in their hearts, nor the love of God shed abroad therein:—Or else they suppose they shall infallibly be so, barely because they use these means; idly dreaming, (though perhaps hardly conscious thereof,) either that there is some kind of *power* therein, whereby, sooner or later, (they know not when,) they shall certainly be made holy; or that there is a sort of *merit* in using them, which will surely move God to give them holiness, or accept them without it.

6. So little do they understand that great foundation of the whole Christian building, "By grace are ye saved:" Ye are saved from your sins, from the guilt and power thereof, ye are restored to the favour and image of

God, not for any works, merits, or de-
servings of yours, but by the free grace, the
mere mercy of God, through the merits of
his well beloved Son: Ye are thus saved, not
by any power, wisdom, or strength, which is
in you, or in any other creature; but merely
through the grace or power of the Holy
Ghost, which worketh all in all.

7. But the main question remains: "We
know this salvation is the gift and the work
of God; but how (may one say who is convinced he hath it not) may I attain thereto?"
If you say, "Believe, and thou shalt be
saved!" he answers, "True; but how shall I
believe?" You reply, "Wait upon God."
"Well; but how am I to wait? In the means
of grace, or out of them? Am I to wait for
the grace of God which bringeth salvation,
by using these means, or by laying them
aside?"

8. It cannot possibly be conceived, that the
word of God should give no direction in so
important a point; or, that the Son of God,
who came down from heaven for us men
and for our salvation, should have left us
undetermined with regard to a question
wherein our salvation is so nearly concerned.

And, in fact, he hath not left us undetermined; he hath shown us the way wherein
we should go. We have only to consult the
oracles of God; to inquire what is written
there; and, if we simply abide by their decision, there can no possible doubt remain.

III. 1. According to this, according to the decision of holy writ, all who desire the grace of God are to wait for it in the means which he hath ordained; in using, not in laying them aside.

And, First, all who desire the grace of God are to wait for it in the way of prayer. This is the express direction of our Lord himself. In his Sermon upon the Mount, after explaining at large wherein religion consists, and describing the main branches of it, he adds, "Ask, and it shall be given you; seek, and ye shall find; knock, and it shall be opened unto you: For every one that asketh receiveth; and he that seeketh findeth; and to him that knocketh it shall be opened." (Matt. vii. 7, 8.) Here we are in the plainest manner directed to ask, in order to, or as a means of, receiving; to seek, in order to find, the grace of God, the pearl of great price; and to knock, to continue asking and seeking, if we would enter into his kingdom.

2. That no doubt might remain, our Lord labours this point in a more peculiar manner. He appeals to every man's own heart: "What man is there of you, who, if his son ask bread, will he give him a stone? Or, if he ask a fish, will he give him a serpent? If ye then, being evil, know how to give good gifts unto your children, how much more shall your Father which is in heaven," the Father of angels and men, the Father of the spirits of all flesh, "give good things to them that ask him?" (Verses 9-11.) Or, as he expresses

himself on another occasion, including all good things in one, "How much more shall your heavenly Father give the Holy Spirit to them that ask him?" (Luke xi. 13.) It should be particularly observed here, that the persons directed to ask had not then received the Holy Spirit: Nevertheless our Lord directs them to use this means, and promises that it should be effectual; that upon asking they should receive the Holy Spirit, from him whose mercy is over all his works.

3. The absolute necessity of using this means, if we would receive any gift from God, yet farther appears from that remarkable passage which immediately precedes these words: "And he said unto them," whom he had just been teaching how to pray, "Which of you shall have a friend, and shall go unto him at midnight, and shall say unto him, Friend, lend me three loaves: And he from within shall answer, Trouble me not; I cannot rise and give thee. I say unto you, though he will not rise and give him, because he is his friend, yet because of his importunity, he will rise, and give him as many as he needeth. And I say unto you, Ask, and it shall be given you." (Luke xi. 5, 7-9.) "Though he will not give him, because he is his friend, yet because of his importunity he will rise and give him as many as he needeth." How could our blessed Lord more plainly declare, that we may receive of God, by this means, by importunately asking, what otherwise we should not receive at all?

4. "He spake also another parable, to this
end, that men ought always to pray, and not
to faint," till through this means they should
receive of God whatsoever petition they
asked of him: "There was in a city a judge
which feared not God, neither regarded
man. And there was a widow in that city,
and she came unto him, saying, Avenge me
of my adversary. And he would not for a
while; but afterwards he said within himself, Though I fear not God, nor regard man,
yet because this widow troubleth me, I will
avenge her, lest, by her continual coming,
she weary me." (Luke xviii. 1–5.) The ap-
plication of this our Lord himself hath
made: "Hear what the unjust judge saith!"
Because she continues to ask, because she
will take no denial, therefore I will avenge
her. "And shall not God avenge his own
elect, which cry day and night unto him? I
tell you he will avenge them speedily," if
they pray end faint not.

5. A direction, equally full and express, to
wait for the blessings of God in private
prayer, together with a positive promise,
that, by this means, we shall obtain the re-
quest of our lips, he hath given us in those
well-known words: "Enter into thy closet,
and, when thou hast shut thy door, pray to
thy Father which is in secret; and thy Father, which seeth in secret, shall reward thee
openly." (Matt. vi. 6.)

6. If it be possible for any direction to be
more clear, it is that which God hath given

us by the Apostle, with regard to prayer of every kind, public or private, and the blessing annexed thereto: "If any of you lack wisdom, let him ask of God, that giveth to all men liberally," (if they ask; otherwise "ye have not, because ye ask not," James iv. 2,) "and upbraideth not; and it shall be given him." (James i. 5.)

If it be objected, "But this is no direction to unbelievers; to them who know not the pardoning grace of God: For the Apostle adds, 'But let him ask in faith;' otherwise, 'let him not think that he shall receive any thing of the Lord:'" I answer, The meaning of the word *faith*, in this place, is fixed by the Apostle himself, as if it were on purpose to obviate this objection, in the words immediately following: "Let him ask in faith, nothing wavering," nothing *doubting*, μηδὲν διακρινόμενος. Not doubting but God heareth his prayer, and will fulfil the desire of his heart.

The gross, blasphemous absurdity of supposing *faith*, in this place, to be taken in the full Christian meaning, appears hence: It is supposing the Holy Ghost to direct a man who knows he has not this faith, (which is here termed *wisdom*,) to ask it of God, with a positive promise that "it shall be given him;" and then immediately to subjoin, that it shall not be given him, unless he have it before he asks for it! But who can bear such a supposition? From this scripture, therefore, as well as those cited above, we must infer, that all who desire the grace of God are to wait for it in the way of prayer.

7. Secondly. All who desire the grace of God are to wait for it in searching the Scriptures.

"Searching the scriptures" as a means of grace

Our Lord's direction, with regard to the use of this means, is likewise plain and clear. "Search the Scriptures," saith he to the unbelieving Jews, "for they testify of me." (John v. 39.) And for this very end did he direct them to search the Scriptures, that they might believe in him.

The objection, that "this is not a command, but only an assertion, that they did search the Scriptures," is shamelessly false. I desire those who urge it, to let us know how a command can be more clearly expressed, than in those terms, ἐραυνᾶτε τὰς γραφάς. It is as peremptory as so many words can make it.

And what a blessing from God attends the use of this means, appears from what is recorded concerning the Bereans; who, after hearing St. Paul, "searched the Scriptures daily, whether those things were so. Therefore many of them believed"—found the grace of God, in the way which he had ordained. (Acts xxvii. 11, 12.)

It is probable, indeed, that in some of those who had "received the word with all readiness of mind," "faith came," as the same Apostle speaks, "by hearing," and was only confirmed by reading the Scriptures: But it was observed above, that under the general

term of searching the Scriptures, both hearing, reading, and meditating are contained.

8. And that this is a means whereby God not
only gives, but also confirms and increases,
true wisdom, we learn from the words of St.
Paul to Timothy: "From a child thou hast
known the Holy Scriptures, which are able
to make thee wise unto salvation through
faith which is in Christ Jesus." (2 Tim. iii.
15.) The same truth (namely, that this is the
great means God has ordained for conveying his manifold grace to man) is delivered,
in the fullest manner that can be conceived,
in the words which immediately follow: "All
Scripture is given by inspiration of God;"
consequently, all Scripture is infallibly true;
"and is profitable for doctrine, for reproof,
for correction, for instruction in righteousness" to the end "that the man of God may
be perfect, thoroughly furnished unto all
good works." (Verses 16,17.)

9. It should be observed, that this is spoken
primarily and directly of the Scriptures
which Timothy had known from a child;
which must have been those of the Old Testament, for the New was not then wrote.
How far then was St. Paul (though he was
"not a whit behind the very chief of the
Apostles," nor, therefore, I presume, behind
any man now upon earth) from making
light of the Old Testament! Behold this, lest
ye one day "wonder and perish," ye who
make so small account of one half of the oracles of God! Yea, and that half of which the

Holy Ghost expressly declares, that it is "profitable," as a means ordained of God, for this very thing, "for doctrine, for reproof, for correction, for instruction in righteousness;" to the end, "the man of God may be perfect, thoroughly furnished unto all good works."

10. Nor is this profitable only for the men of God, for those who walk already in the light of his countenance; but also for those who are yet in darkness, seeking him whom they know not. Thus St. Peter, "We have also a more sure word of prophecy:" Literally, "And we have the prophetic word more sure;" Καὶ ἔχομεν βεβαιότερον τὸν προφητικὸν λόγον confirmed by our being "eye-witnesses of his Majesty," and "hearing the voice which came from the excellent glory;" unto which—prophetic word; so he styles the Holy Scriptures—"ye do well that ye take heed, as unto a light that shineth in a dark place, until the day dawn, and the Day-star arise in your hearts." (2 Peter i. 19.) Let all, therefore, who desire that day to dawn upon their hearts, wait for it in searching the Scriptures.

11. Thirdly. All who desire an increase of the grace of God are to wait for it in partaking of the Lord's supper: For this also is a direction himself hath given. "The same night in which he was betrayed, he took bread, and brake it, and said, Take, eat; this is my body;" that is, the sacred sign of my body: "This do in remembrance of me." Likewise,

The Lord's Supper as a means of grace

"he took the cup, saying, This cup is the new testament," or covenant, "in my blood;" the sacred sign of that covenant; "this do ye in remembrance of me." "For as often as ye eat this bread, and drink this cup, ye do show forth the Lord's death till he come:" (1 Cor. xi. 23, &c.:) Ye openly exhibit the same, by these visible signs, before God, and angels, and men; ye manifest your solemn remembrance of his death, till he cometh in the clouds of heaven.

Only "let a man" first "examine himself," whether he understand the nature and design of this holy institution, and whether he really desire to be himself made conformable to the death of Christ; and so, nothing doubting, "let him eat of that bread, and drink of that cup." (Verse 28.)

Here, then, the direction first given by our Lord is expressly repeated by the Apostle: "Let him eat; let him drink;" (ἐσθιέτω, πινέτω, both in the imperative mood) words not implying a bare permission only, but a clear, explicit command; a command to all those who either already are filled with peace and joy in believing, or can truly say, "The remembrance of our sins is grievous unto us, the burden of them is intolerable."

12. And that this is also an ordinary, stated means of receiving the grace of God, is evident from those words of the Apostle, which occur in the preceding chapter: "The cup of blessing which we bless, is it not the com-

munion," or *communication*, "of the blood
of Christ? The bread which we break, is it
not the communion of the body of Christ?"
(1 Cor. x. 16.) Is not the eating of that bread,
and the drinking of that cup, the outward,
visible means, whereby God conveys into
our souls all that spiritual grace, that righteousness, and peace, and joy in the Holy
Ghost, which were purchased by the body of
Christ once broken and the blood of Christ
once shed for us? Let all, therefore, who
truly desire the grace of God, eat of that
bread, and drink of that cup.

IV. 1. But as plainly as God hath pointed out
the way wherein he will be inquired after,
innumerable are the objections which men,
wise in their own eyes, have, from time to
time, raised against it. It may be needful to
consider a few of these; not because they are
of weight in themselves, but because they
have so often been used, especially of late
years, to turn the lame out of the way; yea,
to trouble and subvert those who did run
well, till Satan appeared as an angel of light.

IV. Answers to objections

The first and chief of these is, "You cannot
use these means (as you call them) without
trusting in them." I pray, where is this written? I expect you should show me plain
Scripture for your assertion: Otherwise I
dare not receive it; because I am not convinced that you are wiser than God.

If it really had been as you assert, it is certain Christ must have known it. And if he
had known it, he would surely have warned

us; he would have revealed it long ago.
Therefore, because he has not, because
there is no tittle of this in the whole revelation of Jesus Christ, I am as fully assured
your assertion is false, as that this revelation
is of God.

"However, leave them off for a short time,
to see whether you trusted in them or no."
So I am to disobey God, in order to know
whether I trust in obeying him! And do you
avow this advice? Do you deliberately teach
to "do evil, that good may come?" O tremble
at the sentence of God against such teachers! Their "damnation is just."

"Nay, if you are troubled when you leave
them off, it is plain you trusted in them." By
no means. If I am troubled when I wilfully
disobey God, it is plain his Spirit is still
striving with me; but if I am not troubled at
wilful sin, it is plain I am given up to a rep-
robate mind.

But what do you mean by "*trusting* in
them?"—looking for the blessing of God
therein? believing, that if I wait in this way,
I shall attain what otherwise I should not?
So I do. And so I will, God being my helper,
even to my life's end. By the grace of God I
will *thus* trust in them, till the day of my
death; that is, I will believe, that whatever
God hath promised, he is faithful also to
perform. And seeing he hath promised to
bless me in this way, I *trust* it shall be according to his word.

2. It has been, Secondly, objected, "This is seeking salvation by works." Do you know the meaning of the expression you use? What is seeking salvation by works? In the writings of St. Paul, it means, either seeking to be saved by observing the ritual works of the Mosaic law; or expecting salvation for the sake of our own works, by the merit of our own righteousness. But how is either of these implied in my waiting in the way God has ordained, and expecting that he will meet me there, because he has promised so to do?

I do expect that he will fulfil his word, that he will meet and bless me in this way. Yet not for the sake of any works which I have done, nor for the merit of my righteousness; but merely through the merits, and sufferings, and love of his Son, in whom he is always well pleased.

3. It has been vehemently objected, Thirdly, "that Christ is the only means of grace." I answer, this is mere playing upon words. Explain your term, and the objection vanishes away. When we say, "Prayer is a means of grace," we understand a channel through which the grace of God is conveyed. When you say, "Christ is the means of grace," you understand the sole price and purchaser of it; or, that "no man cometh unto the Father, but through him." And who denies it? But this is utterly wide of the question.

4. "But does not the Scripture" (it has been objected, Fourthly) "direct us to *wait* for salvation? Does not David say, 'My soul waiteth upon God, for of him cometh my salvation?' And does not Isaiah teach us the same thing, saying, 'O Lord, we have waited for thee?'" All this cannot be denied. Seeing it is the gift of God, we are undoubtedly to *wait* on him for salvation. But how shall we wait? If God himself has appointed a way, can you find a better way of waiting for him? But that he hath appointed a way hath been shown at large, and also what that way is. The very words of the Prophet, which you cite, put this out of all question. For the whole sentence runs thus:—"In the way of thy judgements," or ordinances, "O Lord, have we waited for thee." (Isaiah xxvi. 8.) And in the very same way did David wait, as his own words abundantly testify: "I have waited for thy saving health, O Lord, and have kept thy law. Teach me, O Lord, the way of thy statutes, and I shall keep it unto the end."

5. "Yea," say some, "but God has appointed another way.—'Stand still, and see the salvation of God.'"

Let us examine the Scriptures to which you refer. The first of them, with the context, runs thus:—

"And when Pharaoh drew nigh, the children of Israel lifted up their eyes; and they were sore afraid. And they said unto Moses, Because there were no graves in Egypt, hast

thou taken us away to die in the wilderness?
And Moses said unto the people, Fear ye
not; stand still, and see the salvation of the
Lord. And the Lord said unto Moses, Speak
unto the children of Israel that they go forward. But lift thou up thy rod, and stretch
out thine hand over the sea, and divide it.
And the children of Israel shall go on dry
ground through the midst of the sea."
(Exod. xiv. 10, &c.)

This was the *salvation of God*, which they
stood still to see, by *marching forward* with
all their might!

The other passage, wherein this expression
occurs, stands thus: "There came some that
told Jehoshaphat, saying, There cometh a
great multitude against thee, from beyond
the sea. And Jehoshaphat feared, and set
himself to seek the Lord, and proclaimed a
fast throughout all Judah. And Judah
gathered themselves together to ask help of
the Lord: Even out of all the cities they
came to seek the Lord. And Jehoshaphat
stood in the congregation, in the house of
the Lord.—Then upon Jahaziel came the
Spirit of the Lord. And he said, Be not dis-
mayed by reason of this great multitude. To-
morrow go ye down against them: Ye shall
not need to fight in this battle. Set
yourselves: Stand ye still, and see the salvation of the Lord. And they rose early in the
morning, and went forth. And then they
began to sing and to praise, the Lord set
ambushments against the children of Moab,

Ammon, and mount Seir:—and every one helped to destroy another." (2 Chron. xx. 2, &c.)

Such was the salvation which the children of Judah saw. But how does all this prove, that we ought not to wait for the grace of God in the means which he hath ordained?

6. I shall mention but one objection more, which, indeed, does not properly belong to this head: Nevertheless, because it has been so frequently urged, I may not wholly pass it by.

"Does not St. Paul say, 'If ye be dead with Christ, why are ye subject to ordinances?' (Col. ii. 20.) Therefore a Christian, one that is dead with Christ, need not use the ordinances any more."

So you say, "If I am a Christian, I am not subject to the ordinances of Christ!" Surely, by the absurdity of this, you must see at the first glance, that the ordinances here mentioned cannot be the ordinances of Christ: That they must needs be the Jewish ordinances, to which it is certain a Christian is no longer subject.

And the same undeniably appears from the words immediately following, "Touch not, taste not, handle not;" all evidently referring to the ancient ordinances of the Jewish law.

So that this objection is the weakest of all. And, in spite of all, that great truth must stand unshaken,—that all who desire the

V. The order and manner of using the means of grace

grace of God, are to wait for it in the means which he hath ordained.

V. 1. But this being allowed, that all who desire the grace of God are to wait for it in the means he hath ordained; it may still be inquired, how those means should be used, both as to the order and the manner of using them.

The order of using the means of grace

With regard to the former, we may observe, there is a kind of order, wherein God himself is generally pleased to use these means in bringing a sinner to salvation. A stupid, senseless wretch is going on in his own way, not having God in all his thoughts, when God comes upon him unawares, perhaps by an awakening sermon or conversation, perhaps by some awful providence, or, it may be, by an immediate stroke of his convincing Spirit, without any outward means at all. Having now a desire to flee from the wrath to come, he purposely goes to *hear* how it may be done. If he finds a preacher who speaks to the heart, he is amazed, and begins searching the Scriptures, whether these things are so? The more he *hears* and *reads*, the more convinced he is; and the more he meditates thereon day and night. Perhaps he finds some other book which explains and enforces what he has heard and read in Scripture. And by all these means, the arrows of conviction sink deeper into his soul. He begins also to *talk* of the things of God, which are ever uppermost in his thoughts; yea, and to talk with God; to *pray* to him; although, through fear and shame, he scarce knows what to say. But whether he can speak or no, he cannot but pray, were it only in "groans which cannot be uttered." Yet, being in doubt, whether "the high and lofty One that inhabiteth eternity" will regard such a sinner as him, he wants to pray with those who know God, with the faithful, in the great congregation. But here he observes others go up to the table of the Lord. He considers, "Christ has said, 'Do this!' How is it that I do not? I am too great a sinner. I am not fit. I am not worthy." After struggling with these scruples awhile, he breaks through. And thus he continues in God's way, in hearing, reading, meditating, praying, and partaking of the Lord's supper, till God, in the manner that pleases him, speaks to his heart, "Thy faith hath saved thee. Go in peace."

2. By observing this order of God, we may learn what means to recommend to any particular soul. If any of these will reach a stupid, careless sinner, it is probably hearing, or conversation. To such, therefore, we might recommend these, if he has ever any thought about salvation. To one who begins to feel the weight of his sins, not only hearing the word of God, but reading it too, and perhaps other serious books, may be a means of deeper conviction. May you not advise him also, to meditate on what he reads, that it may have its full force upon his heart? Yea, and to speak thereof, and not be ashamed, particularly among those who

walk in the same path. When trouble and heaviness take hold upon him, should you not then earnestly exhort him to pour out his soul before God; "always to pray and not to faint;" and when he feels the worthlessness of his own prayers, are you not to work together with God, and remind him of going up into the house of the Lord, and praying with all that fear him? But if he does this, the dying word of his Lord will soon be brought to his remembrance; a plain intimation, that this is the time when we should second the motions of the blessed Spirit. And thus may we lead him, step by step, through all the means which God has ordained; not according to our own will, but just as the Providence and the Spirit of God go before and open the way.

3. Yet, as we find no command in holy writ for any particular order to be observed herein, so neither do the providence and the Spirit of God adhere to any without variation; but the means into which different men are led, and in which they find the blessing of God, are varied, transposed, and combined together, a thousand different ways. Yet still our wisdom is to follow the leadings of his providence and his Spirit; to be guided herein, (more especially as to the means wherein we ourselves seek the grace of God,) partly by his outward providence, giving us the opportunity of using sometimes one means, sometimes another, partly by our experience, which it is whereby his free Spirit is pleased most to work in our

heart. And in the mean time, the sure and general rule for all who groan for the salvation of God is this,—whenever opportunity serves, use all the means which God has ordained; for who knows in which God will meet thee with the grace that bringeth salvation?

4. As to the manner of using them, whereon indeed it wholly depends whether they shall convey any grace at all to the user; it behooves us, First, always to retain a lively sense, that God is above all means. Have a care, therefore, of limiting the Almighty. He doeth whatsoever and whensoever it pleaseth him. He can convey his grace, either in or out of any of the means which he hath appointed. Perhaps he will. "Who hath known the mind of the Lord? or who hath been his counsellor?" Look then every moment for his appearing! Be it at the hour you are employed in his ordinances; or before, or after that hour; or when you are hindered therefrom. He is not hindered; He is always ready, always able, always willing to save. "It is the Lord: Let him do what seemeth him good!"

The manner of using the means of grace

Secondly. Before you use any means, let it be deeply impressed on your soul,—there is no *power* in this. It is, in itself, a poor, dead, empty thing: Separate from God, it is a dry leaf, a shadow. Neither is there any *merit* in my using this; nothing intrinsically pleasing to God; nothing whereby I deserve any favour at his hands, no, not a drop of water to cool my tongue. But, because God bids, therefore I do; because he directs me to wait in this way, therefore here I wait for his free mercy, whereof cometh my salvation.

Settle this in your heart, that the *opus operatum*, the mere *work done*, profiteth nothing; that there is no *power* to save, but in the Spirit of God, no *merit*, but in the blood of Christ; that, consequently, even what God ordains, conveys no grace to the soul, if you trust not in Him alone. On the other hand, he that does truly trust in Him, cannot fall short of the grace of God, even though he were cut off from every outward ordinance, though he were shut up in the centre of the earth.

Thirdly. In using all means, seek God alone. In and through every outward thing, look singly to the *power* of his Spirit, and the *merits* of his Son. Beware you do not stick in the *work* itself; if you do, it is all lost labour. Nothing short of God can satisfy your soul. Therefore, eye him in all, through all, and above all.

Remember also, to use all means, *as means*; as ordained, not for their own sake, but in order to the renewal of your soul in righteousness and true holiness. If, therefore, they actually tend to this, well; but if not, they are dung and dross.

Lastly. After you have used any of these, take care how you value yourself thereon: How you congratulate yourself as having done some great thing. This is turning all into poison. Think, "If God was not there, what does this avail? Have I not been adding sin to sin? How long? O Lord! save, or I perish! O lay not this sin to my charge!" If God was there, if his love flowed into your heart, you have forgot, as it were, the outward work. You see, you know, you feel, God is all in all. Be abased. Sink down before him. Give him all the praise. "Let God in all things be glorified through Christ Jesus." Let all your bones cry out, "My song shall be always of the loving kindness of the Lord: With my mouth will I ever be telling of thy truth, from one generation to another!"

CHARLES WESLEY, HYMNS
"TO–JESUS, SHEW US THY SALVATION"
AND "THE GREAT SUPPER" (1747)

Comment: The first hymn in this collection from 1747, "To–Jesus, Shew Us Thy Salvation," describes Charles Wesley's poetic vision of Christian perfection or entire sanctification, the point when a believer comes to love God completely, that is, with all one's heart, soul, mind, and strength. Divine love, in the view of this hymn, is thus not only the beginning point ("alpha") for the Christian life, it is also the end towards which ("omega") the Christian life is directed by divine grace. The hymn is well known to Methodists and is sometimes sung at weddings, though this use may reflect a serious misunderstanding of the kind of love Charles Wesley describes in this hymn.

The second hymn from this 1747 collection was designed as a hymn celebrating Christ's grace available in the sacrament of holy communion, but Methodist churches have often selected verses from it that extend an evangelical "invitation" to sinners without verses that explicitly deal with holy communion. The current hymnal of The United Methodist Church actually has two hymns based on this text: one extending the evangelical invitation (no. 339) and one celebrating Christ's grace and presence in the Lord's supper (no. 616). Perhaps most importantly, the hymn makes abundantly clear the Wesleys' commitment to teach that God's grace is available universally, that is, to all human beings ("Let every soul be Jesu's guest"). This consistent teaching implicitly rejects the notion that saving grace is available only to a limit number of the those who are elect or predestined to salvation.

Source: These hymns were originally published in a collection of *Hymns for Those that Seek, and Those that Have Redemption in the Blood of Jesus Christ* (1747, pp. 13-14 and 65-68). The versions cited here are from Osborn, *Poetical Works*, 4:219-220 and 4:274-277).

To–Jesus, Shew Us Thy Salvation

Love Divine, all loves excelling,
Joy of heaven, to earth come down,
Fix in us Thy humble dwelling,
All Thy faithful mercies crown:
Jesu, Thou art all compassion,
Pure, unbounded love Thou art,
Visit us with Thy salvation,
Enter every trembling heart.

Breathe, O breathe Thy loving Spirit,
Into every troubled breast,
Let us all in Thee inherit,
Let us find that second rest:
Take away our power of sinning,
Alpha and Omega be,
End of faith as its Beginning,
Set our hearts at liberty.

Come, almighty to deliver,
Let us all Thy life receive;
Suddenly return, and never,
Never more Thy temples leave.
Thee we would be always blessing,
Serve Thee as Thy hosts above,

Pray, and praise Thee without ceasing,
Glory in Thy perfect love.

Finish then Thy new creation,
Pure, and spotless let us be,
Let us see Thy great salvation,
Perfectly restored in Thee:
Changed from glory into glory,
Till in heaven we take our place,
Till we cast our crowns before Thee,
Lost in wonder, love, and praise!

The Great Supper

Come, sinners, to the gospel feast,
Let every soul be Jesu's guest,
You need not one be left behind,
For God hath bidden all mankind.

Sent by my Lord, on you I call,
The invitation is to all,
Come all the world; come, sinner, thou,
All things in Christ are ready now.

Jesus to you His fulness brings,
A feast of marrow and fat things:
All, all in Christ is freely given,
Pardon, and holiness, and heaven.

Do not begin to make excuse,
Ah! do not you His grace refuse;
Your worldly cares and pleasures leave,
And take what Jesus hath to give.

Your grounds forsake, your oxen quit,
Your every earthly thought forget,
Seek not the comforts of this life,
Nor sell your Saviour for a wife.

"Have me excused," why will ye say?
Why will ye for damnation pray?
Have you excused—from joy and peace!
Have you excused—from happiness:

Excused from coming to a feast!
Excused from being Jesu's guest!
From knowing now your sins forgiven,
From tasting here the joys of heaven!

Excused, alas! why should you be
From health, and life, and liberty,
From entering into glorious rest,
From leaning on your Saviour's breast!

Yet must I, Lord, to Thee complain,
The world hath made Thy offers vain;
Too busy, or too happy they,
They will not, Lord, Thy call obey.

Go then, my angry Master said,
Since these on all My mercies tread,
Invite the rich and great no more,
But preach My gospel to the poor.

Confer not thou with flesh and blood,
Go quickly forth, invite the crowd,
Search every lane, and every street,
And bring in all the souls you meet.

Come then, ye souls by sin opprest,
Ye restless wanderers after rest,
Ye poor, and maim'd, and halt, and blind,
In Christ a hearty welcome find.

Sinners my gracious Lord receives,
Harlots, and publicans, and thieves;
Drunkards, and all ye hellish crew,
I have a message now to you.

Come, and partake the gospel feast,
Be saved from sin, in Jesus rest:
O taste the goodness of our God,
And eat His flesh, and drink His blood.

'Tis done: my all-redeeming Lord,
I have gone forth, and preach'd the word,
The sinners to Thy feast are come,
And yet, O Saviour, there is room.

Go then, my Lord again enjoin'd,
And other wandering sinners find;
Go to the hedges and highways,
And offer all My pardoning grace.

The worst unto My supper press,
Monsters of daring wickedness,
Tell them My grace for all is free,
They cannot be too bad for Me.

Tell them, their sins are all forgiven,
Tell every creature under heaven
I died to save them from all sin,
And force the vagrants to come in.

Ye vagrant souls, on you I call,
(O that my voice could reach you all!)
Ye all are freely justified,
Ye all may live, for Christ hath died.

My message as from God receive,
Ye all may come to Christ, and live:
O let His love your hearts constrain,
Nor suffer Him to die in vain.

His love is mighty to compel,
His conquering love consent to feel;
Yield to His love's resistless power,
And fight against your God no more!

See Him set forth before your eyes,
Behold the bleeding Sacrifice!
His offer'd love make haste to' embrace,
And freely now be saved by grace.

Ye who believe His record true
Shall sup with Him, and He with you:
Come to the feast; be saved from sin,
For Jesus waits to take you in.

This is the time, no more delay,
This is the acceptable day,
Come in, this moment, at His call,
And live for Him who died for all.

ITEM 11:

JOHN WESLEY,
SERMON ON A "CATHOLIC SPIRIT" (1749)

Comment: John Wesley took the view that, although a Christian needs to be firmly committed to basic, shared Christian beliefs ("the main branches of Christian doctrine"), their differences over "opinions" or "modes of worship," which have often been critical dividing points for Christians, should not keep them from loving each other. He called this attitude a "catholic spirit," and this sermon urges Christians to have just such a spirit or attitude of openness or liberality towards their fellow Christians. The sermon comes from a year (1749) notable for John Wesley's attempts to patch up relationships with Calvinistic Evangelicals, on the one hand, and with Irish Catholics amongst whom he was ministering, on the other (and see the next item from the same year).

Source: Jackson, *Works*, 5:492-504.

"And when he was departed thence, he lighted on Jehonadab the son of Rechab coming to meet him, and he saluted him, and said to him, Is thine heart right, as my heart is with thy heart? And Jehonadab answered: It is. If it be, give me thine hand." 2 Kings x. 15.

1. IT is allowed even by those who do not pay this great debt, that love is due to all mankind, the royal law, "Thou shalt love thy neighbour as thyself," carrying its own evid-

Introduction

ence to all that hear it: and that, not accord- The universal obligation
ing to the miserable construction put upon of love for one's fellow human beings
it by the zealots of old times, "Thou shalt
love thy neighbour," thy relation, acquaintance, friend, "and hate thine enemy;" not
so; "I say unto you," said our Lord, "Love
your enemies, bless them that curse you, do
good to them that hate you, and pray for
them that despitefully use you, and persecute you; that ye may be the children," may
appear so to all mankind, "of your Father
which is in heaven; who maketh his sun to
rise on the evil and on the good, and send-
eth rain on the just and on the unjust."

2. But it is sure, there is a peculiar love This sermon will focus
which we owe to those that love God. So on love between Christians
David: "All my delight is upon the saints
that are in the earth, and upon such as excel
in virtue." And so a greater than he: "A new
commandment I give unto you, That ye love
one another: as I have loved you, that ye
also love one another. By this shall all men
know that ye are my disciples, if ye have
love one to another" (John xiii. 34, 35). This
is that love on which the Apostle John so
frequently and strongly insists: "This," saith
he, "is the message that ye heard from the
beginning, that we should love one another"
(1 John iii. 11). "Hereby perceive we the love
of God, because he laid down his life for us:
and we ought," if love should call us thereto,
"to lay down our lives for the brethren"
(Verse 16). And again: "Beloved, let us love
one another: For love is of God. He that
loveth not, knoweth not God; for God is

love" (iv. 7, 8). "Not that we loved God, but that he loved us, and sent his Son to be the propitiation for our sins. Beloved, if God so loved us, we ought also to love one another." (Verses 10, 11).

3. All men approve of this; but do all men practise it? Daily experience shows the contrary. Where are even the Christians who "love one another as he hath given us commandment?" How many hindrances lie in the way! The two grand, general hindrances are, First, that they cannot all think alike; and, in consequence of this, Secondly, they cannot all walk alike; but in several smaller points their practice must differ in proportion to the difference of their sentiments.

4. But although a difference in opinions or modes of worship may prevent an entire external union; yet need it prevent our union in affection? Though we cannot think alike, may we not love alike? May we not be of one heart, though we are not of one opinion? Without all doubt, we may. Herein all the children of God may unite, notwithstanding these smaller differences. These remaining as they are, they may forward one another in love and in good works.

5. Surely in this respect the example of Jehu himself, as mixed a character as he was of, is well worthy both the attention and imitation of every serious Christian. "And when he was departed thence, he lighted on Jehonadab the son of Rechab coming to meet him. And he saluted him, and said to him, Is

thine heart right, as my heart is with thy heart? And Jehonadab answered, It is. If it be, give me thine hand."

The text naturally divides itself into two parts:—First, a question proposed by Jehu to Jehonadab: "Is thine heart right, as my heart is with thy heart?" Secondly, an offer made on Jehonadab's answering, "It is:"—"If it be, give me thine hand."

I. 1. And, first, let us consider the question proposed by Jehu to Jehonadab, "Is thine heart right, as my heart is with thy heart?"

I What is involved in being of one heart with other Christians?

Being of one heart does not depend on unity in "opinions"

The very first thing we may observe in these words, is, that here is no inquiry concerning Jehonadab's opinions. And yet it is certain, he held some which were very uncommon, indeed quite peculiar to himself; and some which had a close influence upon his practice; on which, likewise, he laid so great a stress, as to entail them upon his children's children, to their latest posterity. This is evident from the account given by Jeremiah many years after his death: "I took Jaazani-ah and his brethren and all his sons, and the whole house of the Rechabites,—and set before them pots full of wine, and cups, and said unto them, Drink ye wine. But they said, We will drink no wine: for Jonadab," or Jehonadab, "the son of Rechab, our father," (it would be less ambiguous, if the words were placed thus: "Jehonadab *our father, the son* of Rechab," out of love and reverence to whom, he probably desired his descendants might be called by his name),

"commanded us, saying, Ye shall drink no
wine, neither ye, nor your sons for ever.
Neither shall ye build house, nor sow seed;
nor plant vineyard, nor have any: but all
your days ye shall dwell in tents.—And we
have obeyed, and done according to all that
Jonadab our father commanded us." (Jer.
xxxv. 3-10.)

2. And yet Jehu (although it seems to have
been his manner both in things secular and
religious, to *drive furiously*) does not con-
cern himself at all with any of these things,
but lets Jehonadab abound in his own
sense. And neither of them appears to have
given the other the least disturbance touching the opinions which he maintained.

3. It is very possible, that many good men
now also may entertain peculiar opinions;
and some of them may be as singular herein
as even Jehonadab was. And it is certain, so
long as we know but *in part*, that all men
will not see all things alike. It is an unavoidable consequence of the present weakness
and shortness of human understanding,
that several men will be of several minds in
religion as well as in common life. So it has
been from the beginning of the world, and
so it will be "till the restitution of all things."

4. Nay, farther: although every man necessarily believes that every particular opinion
which he holds is true (for to believe any
opinion is not true, is the same thing as not
to hold it); yet can no man be assured that
all his own opinions, taken together, are

true. Nay, every thinking man is assured
they are not, seeing *humanum est errare et
nescire*: "To be ignorant of many things,
and to mistake in some, is the necessary
condition of humanity." This, therefore, he
is sensible, is his own case. He knows, in the
general, that he himself is mistaken; although in what particulars he mistakes, he
does not, perhaps he cannot, know.

5. I say "perhaps he cannot know;" for who
can tell how far invincible ignorance may
extend? or (that comes to the same thing)
invincible prejudice?—which is often so
fixed in tender minds, that it is afterwards
impossible to tear up what has taken so
deep a root. And who can say, unless he
knew every circumstance attending it, how
far any mistake is culpable? seeing all guilt
must suppose some concurrence of the will;
of which he only can judge who searcheth
the heart.

6. Every wise man, therefore, will allow others the same liberty of thinking which he
desires they should allow him; and will no
more insist on their embracing his opinions,
than he would have them to insist on his
embracing theirs. He bears with those who
differ from him, and only asks him with
whom he desires to unite in love that single
question, "Is thy heart right, as my heart is
with thy heart?"

7. We may, Secondly, observe, that here is
no inquiry made concerning Jehonadab's
mode of worship; although it is highly prob-

Being of one heart does
not depend on unity in
"modes of worship"

able there was, in this respect also, a very
wide difference between them. For we may
well believe Jehonadab, as well as all his
posterity, worshipped God at Jerusalem:
Whereas Jehu did not: he had more regard
to state-policy than religion. And, therefore,
although he slew the worshippers of Baal,
and destroyed Baal out of Israel; yet from
the convenient sin of Jeroboam, the worship of the golden calves, he "departed not."
(2 Kings x. 29.)

8. But even among men of an upright heart,
men who desire to "have a conscience void
of offence," it must needs be, that, as long as
there are various opinions, there will be
various ways of worshipping God; seeing a
variety of opinion necessarily implies a variety of practice. And as, in all ages, men have
differed in nothing more than in their opinions concerning the Supreme Being, so in
nothing have they more differed from each
other, than in the manner of worshipping
him. Had this been only in the heathen
world, it would not have been at all surprising: for we know, these "by" their "wisdom
knew not God;" nor, therefore, could they
know how to worship him. But is it not
strange, that even in the Christian world, although they all agree in the general, "God is
a Spirit; and they that worship him must
worship him in spirit and in truth;" yet the
particular modes of worshipping God are almost as various as among the Heathens?

9. And how shall we choose among so much variety? No man can choose for, or prescribe to, another. But every one must follow the dictates of his own conscience, in simplicity and godly sincerity. He must be fully persuaded in his own mind and then act according to the best light he has. Nor has any creature power to constrain another to walk by his own rule. God has given no right to any of the children of men thus to lord it over the conscience of his brethren; but every man must judge for himself, as every man must give an account of himself to God.

10. Although, therefore, every follower of Christ is obliged, by the very nature of the Christian institution, to be a member of some particular congregation or other, some Church, as it is usually termed (which implies a particular manner of worshipping God; for "two cannot walk together unless they be agreed"); yet none can be obliged by any power on earth but that of his own conscience, to prefer this or that congregation to another, this or that particular manner of worship. I know it is commonly supposed, that the place of our birth fixes the Church to which we ought to belong; that one, for instance, who is born in England, ought to be a member of that which is styled the Church of England; and consequently, to worship God in the particular manner which is prescribed by that Church. I was once a zealous maintainer of this; but I find many reasons to abate of this zeal. I fear it is

Such unity does presume commitment to some Church

attended with such difficulties as no reasonable man can get over. Not the least of which is, that if this rule had took place, there could have been no Reformation from Popery; seeing it entirely destroys the right of private judgement, on which that whole Reformation stands.

11. I dare not, therefore, presume to impose my mode of worship on any other. I believe it is truly primitive and apostolical: But my belief is no rule for another. I ask not, therefore, of him with whom I would unite in love, Are you of my Church, of my congregation? Do you receive the same form of Church government, and allow the same Church officers, with me? Do you join in the same form of prayer wherein I worship God? I inquire not, Do you receive the supper of the Lord in the same posture and manner that I do? nor whether, in the administration of baptism, you agree with me in admitting sureties for the baptised; in the manner of administering it; or the age of those to whom it should be administered. Nay, I ask not of you (as clear as I am in my own mind), whether you allow baptism and the Lord's supper at all. Let all these things stand by: we will talk of them, if need be, at a more convenient season, my only question at present is this, "Is thine heart right, as my heart is with thy heart?"

12. But what is properly implied in the question? I do not mean, What did Jehu imply therein? But, what should a follower of

Christ understand thereby, when he proposes it to any of his brethren?

The first thing implied is this: Is thy heart right with God? Dost thou believe his being and his perfections? his eternity, immensity, wisdom, power; his justice, mercy, and truth? Dost thou believe that he now "upholdeth all things by the word of his power?" and that he governs even the most minute, even the most noxious, to his own glory, and the good of them that love him? Hast thou a divine evidence, a supernatural conviction, of the things of God? Dost thou "walk by faith, not by sight?" looking not at temporal things, but things eternal?

Such unity involves belief in and commitment to God

13. Dost thou believe in the Lord Jesus Christ, "God over all, blessed for ever?" Is he revealed in thy soul? Dost thou know Jesus Christ and him crucified? Does he dwell in thee, and thou in him? Is he formed in thy heart by faith? Having absolutely disclaimed all thy own works, thy own righteousness, hast thou "submitted thyself unto the righteousness of God," which is by faith in Christ Jesus? Art thou "found in him, not having thy own righteousness, but the righteousness which is by faith?" And art thou, through him, "fighting the good fight of faith, and laying hold of eternal life?"

Such unity involves belief in and commitment to Jesus Christ

14. Is thy faith ἐνεργουμένη δι' ἀγάπης,— *filled with the energy of love?* Dost thou love God (I do not say "above all things," for it is both an unscriptural and an ambiguous expression, but) "with all thy heart, and

Such unity involves true, living faith

with all thy mind, and with all thy soul, and with all thy strength?" Dost thou seek all thy happiness in him alone? And dost thou find what thou seekest? Does thy soul continually "magnify the Lord, and thy spirit rejoice in God thy Saviour?" Having learned "in everything to give thanks," dost thou find "it is a joyful and a pleasant thing to be thankful?" Is God the centre of thy soul? the sum of all thy desires? Art thou accordingly laying up thy treasure in heaven, and counting all things else dung and dross? Hath the love of God cast the love of the world out of thy soul? Then thou art "crucified to the world;" thou art dead to all below; and thy "life is hid with Christ in God."

15. Art thou employed in doing, "not thy own will, but the will of him that sent thee"—of him that sent thee down to sojourn here awhile, to spend a few days in a strange land, till, having finished the work he hath given thee to do, thou return to thy Father's house? Is it thy meat and drink "to do the will of thy Father which is in heaven?" Is thine eye single in all things? always fixed on him? always looking unto Jesus? Dost thou point at him in whatsoever thou doest? in all thy labour, thy business, thy conversation? aiming only at the glory of God in all;—"whatsoever thou doest, either in word or deed, doing it all in the name of the Lord Jesus; giving thanks unto God, even the Father, through him?"

Such unity involves doing God's will

16. Does the love of God constrain thee to serve him with fear?—to "rejoice unto him with reverence?" Art thou more afraid of displeasing God, than either of death or hell? Is nothing so terrible to thee as the thought of offending the eyes of his glory? Upon this ground, dost thou "hate all evil ways," every transgression of his holy and perfect law; and herein "exercise thyself, to have a conscience void of offence toward God, and toward man?"

Such unity involves fear of displeasing God by sin

17. Is thy heart right toward thy neighbour? Dost thou love, as thyself, all mankind, without exception? "If you love those only that love you, what thank have ye?" Do you "love your enemies?" Is your soul full of good-will, of tender affection, toward them? Do you love even the enemies of God, the unthankful and unholy? Do your bowels yearn over them? Could you "wish yourself" temporally "accursed" for their sake? And do you show this by "blessing them that curse you, and praying for those that des-pitefully use you, and persecute you?"

Such unity involves love for our neighbor

18. Do you show your love by your works? While you have time, as you have opportun-ity, do you in fact "do good to all men," neighbours or strangers, friends or enemies, good or bad? Do you do them all the good you can; endeavouring to supply all their wants; assisting them both in body and soul, to the uttermost of your power?—If thou art thus minded, may every Christian say, yea, if thou art but sincerely desirous of

Such unity involves commitment that is shown through good works

it, and following on till thou attain, then "thy heart is right, as my heart is with thy heart."

II. 1. "If it be, give me thy hand." I do not mean, "Be of my opinion." You need not: I do not expect or desire it. Neither do I mean, "I will be of your opinion." I cannot: It does not depend on my choice: I can no more think, than I can see or hear, as I will. Keep you your opinion; I mine; and that as steadily as ever. You need not even endeavour to come over to me, or bring me over to you. I do not desire you to dispute those points, or to hear or speak one word concerning them. Let all opinions alone on one side and the other: only "give me thine hand."

II. What is further implied in being of one heart with other Christians?

2. I do not mean, "Embrace my modes of worship," or, "I will embrace yours." This also is a thing which does not depend either on your choice or mine. We must both act as each is fully persuaded in his own mind. Hold you fast that which you believe is most acceptable to God, and I will do the same. I believe the Episcopal form of church government to be scriptural and apostolical. If you think the Presbyterian or Independent is better, think so still, and act accordingly. I believe infants ought to be baptised; and that this may be done either by dipping or sprinkling. If you are otherwise persuaded, be so still, and follow your own persuasion. It appears to me, that forms of prayer are of excellent use, particularly in the great con-

It does not imply embracing the modes of worship of another Christian community

gregation. If you judge extemporary prayer to be of more use, act suitable to your own judgement. My sentiment is, that I ought not to forbid water, wherein persons may be baptised; and that I ought to eat bread and drink wine, as a memorial of my dying Master: However, if you are not convinced of this, act according to the light you have. I have no desire to dispute with you one moment upon any of the preceding heads. Let all these smaller points stand aside. Let them never come into sight "If thine heart is as my heart," if thou lovest God and all mankind, I ask no more: "Give me thine hand."

3. I mean, First, love me: And that not only as thou lovest all mankind; not only as thou lovest thine enemies, or the enemies of God, those that hate thee, that "despitefully use thee, and persecute thee;" not only as a stranger, as one of whom thou knowest neither good nor evil;—I am not satisfied with this;—no; "if thine heart be right, as mine with thy heart," then love me with a very tender affection, as a friend that is closer than a brother; as a brother in Christ, a fellow citizen of the New Jerusalem, a fellow soldier engaged in the same warfare, under the same Captain of our salvation. Love me as a companion in the kingdom and patience of Jesus, and a joint heir of his glory.

It implies love for one's fellow Chrstian

4. Love me (but in a higher degree than thou dost the bulk of mankind) with the

love that is *long-suffering and kind*; that is patient; if I am ignorant or out of the way, bearing and not increasing my burden; and is tender, soft, and compassionate still;— that *envieth not*, if at any time it please God to prosper me in his work even more than thee. Love me with the love that *is not provoked*, either at my follies or infirmities; or even at my acting (if it should sometimes so appear to thee) not according to the will of God. Love me so as to *think no evil* of me; to put away all jealousy and evil-surmising. Love me with the love that *covereth all things*; that never reveals either my faults or infirmities,—that *believeth all things*; is always willing to think the best, to put the fairest construction on all my words and actions,—that *hopeth all things*; either that the thing related was never done; or not done with such circumstances as are related; or, at least, that it was done with a good intention, or in a sudden stress of temptation. And hope to the end, that whatever is amiss, will, by the grace of God, be corrected; and whatever is wanting, supplied, through the riches of his mercy in Christ Jesus.

It involves correcting each other and a willingness to be corrected by each other

5. I mean, Secondly, commend me to God in all thy prayers; wrestle with him in my behalf, that he would speedily correct what he sees amiss, and supply what is wanting in me. In thy nearest access to the throne of grace, beg of him who is then very present with thee, that my heart may be more as thy heart, more right both toward God and to-

It involves praying for our fellow Christians

ward man; that I may have a fuller conviction of things not seen, and a stronger view
of the love of God in Christ Jesus; may more
steadily walk by faith, not by sight; and
more earnestly grasp eternal life. Pray that
the love of God and of all mankind may be
more largely poured into my heart; that I
may be more fervent and active in doing the
will of my Father which is in heaven, more
zealous of good works, and more careful to
abstain from all appearance of evil.

6. I mean, Thirdly, provoke me to love and
to good works. Second thy prayer, as thou
hast opportunity, by speaking to me, in love,
whatsoever thou believest to be for my
soul's health. Quicken me in the work which
God has given me to do, and instruct me
how to do it more perfectly. Yea, "smite me
friendly, and reprove me," whereinsoever I
appear to thee to be doing rather my own
will, than the will of him that sent me. O
speak and spare not, whatever thou believest may conduce, either to the amending
my faults, the strengthening my weakness,
the building me up in love, or the making
me more fit, in any kind, for the Master's
use.

It means encouraging each other in good works

7. I mean, Lastly, love me not in word only,
but in deed and in truth. So far as in conscience thou canst (retaining still thy own
opinions, and thy own manner of worshipping God), join with me in the work of God;
and let us go on hand in hand. And thus far,
it is certain, thou mayest go. Speak honour-

It means working with each other and helping each other

ably, wherever thou art, of the work of God,
by whomsoever he works, and kindly of his
messengers. And, if it be in thy power, not
only sympathise with them when they are in
any difficulty or distress, but give them a
cheerful and effectual assistance, that they
may glorify God on thy behalf.

8. Two things should be observed with regard to what has been spoken under this
last head: the one, that whatsoever love,
whatsoever offices of love, whatsoever spiritual or temporal assistance, I claim from
him whose heart is right, as my heart is with
his, the same I am ready, by the grace of
God, according to my measure, to give him:
The other, that I have not made this claim
in behalf of myself only, but of all whose
heart is right toward God and man, that we
may all love one another as Christ hath
loved us.

III. 1. One inference we may make from
what has been said. We may learn from
hence, what is a catholic spirit.

**III. What is a
"catholic spirit"?**

There is scarce any expression which has
been more grossly misunderstood, and
more dangerously misapplied, than this:
But it will be easy for any who calmly consider the preceding observations, to correct
any such misapprehensions of it, and to
prevent any such misapplication.

For, from hence we may learn, First, that a
catholic spirit is not *speculative* latitudinarianism. It is not an indifference to all

opinions: This is the spawn of hell, not the offspring of heaven. This unsettledness of thought, this being "driven to and fro, and tossed about with every wind of doctrine," is a great curse, not a blessing, an irreconcilable enemy, not a friend, to true catholicism. A man of a truly catholic spirit has not now his religion to seek. He is fixed as the sun in his judgement concerning the main branches of Christian doctrine. It is true, he is always ready to hear and weigh whatsoever can be offered against his principles; but as this does not show any wavering in his own mind, so neither does it occasion any. He does not halt between two opinions, nor vainly endeavour to blend them into one. Observe this, you who know not what spirit ye are of; who call yourselves men of a catholic spirit, only because you are of a muddy understanding; because your mind is all in a mist; because you have no settled, consistent principles, but are for jumbling all opinions together. Be convinced, that you have quite missed your way; you know not where you are. You think you are got into the very spirit of Christ; when, in truth, you are nearer the spirit of Antichrist. Go, first, and learn the first elements of the gospel of Christ, and then shall you learn to be of a truly catholic spirit.

> It is not an indifference to differing opinions and it presupposes commitment to "the main branches of Christian doctrine"

2. From what has been said, we may learn, secondly, that a catholic spirit is not any kind of *practical* latitudinarianism. It is not indifference as to public worship, or as to the outward manner of performing it. This,

> It is not an indifference concerning Christian practices

likewise, would not be a blessing but a curse. Far from being an help thereto, it would, so long as it remained, be an unspeakable hindrance to the worshipping of God in spirit and in truth. But the man of a truly catholic spirit, having weighed all things in the balance of the sanctuary, has no doubt, no scruple at all, concerning that particular mode of worship wherein he joins. He is clearly convinced, that this manner of worshipping God is both scriptural and rational. He knows none in the world which is more scriptural, none which is more rational. Therefore, without rambling hither and thither, he cleaves close thereto, and praises God for the opportunity of so doing.

3. Hence we may, Thirdly, learn, that a catholic spirit is not indifference to all congregations. This is another sort of latitudinarianism, no less absurd and unscriptural than the former. But it is far from a man of a truly catholic spirit. He is fixed in his congregation as well as his principles. He is united to one, not only in spirit, but by all the outward ties of Christian fellowship. There he partakes of all the ordinances of God. There he receives the supper of the Lord. There he pours out his soul in public prayer, and joins in public praise and thanksgiving. There he rejoices to hear the word of reconciliation, the gospel of the grace of God. With these his nearest, his best-beloved brethren, on solemn occasions, he seeks God by fasting. These partic-

> It is not an indifference to the differences between Christian churches

ularly he watches over in love, as they do over his soul; admonishing, exhorting, comforting, reproving, and every way building up each other in the faith. These he regards as his own household; and therefore, according to the ability God has given him, naturally cares for them, and provides that they may have all the things that are needful for life and godliness.

4. But while he is steadily fixed in his religious principles in what he believes to be the truth as it is in Jesus; while he firmly adheres to that worship of God which he judges to be most acceptable in his sight; and while he is united by the tenderest and closest ties to one particular congregation,— his heart is enlarged toward all mankind, those he knows and those he does not; he embraces with strong and cordial affection neighbours and strangers, friends and enemies. This is catholic or universal love. And he that has this is of a catholic spirit. For love alone gives the title to this character: Catholic love is a catholic spirit.

A catholic spirit involves catholic or universal love

5. If, then, we take this word in the strictest sense, a man of a catholic spirit is one who, in the manner above-mentioned, gives his hand to all whose hearts are right with his heart: One who knows how to value, and praise God for, all the advantages he enjoys, with regard to the knowledge of the things of God, the true scriptural manner of worshipping him, and, above all, his union with a congregation fearing God and working

righteousness: One who, retaining these
blessings with the strictest care, keeping
them as the apple of his eye, at the same
time loves,—as friends, as brethren in the
Lord, as members of Christ and children of
God, as joint partakers now of the present
kingdom of God, and fellow-heirs of his
eternal kingdom—all, of whatever opinion
or worship, or congregation, who believe in
the Lord Jesus Christ; who love God and
man; who, rejoicing to please, and fearing to
offend God, are careful to abstain from evil,
and zealous of good works. He is the man of
a truly catholic spirit, who bears all these
continually upon his heart; who having an
unspeakable tenderness for their persons,
and longing for their welfare, does not cease
to commend them to God in prayer, as well
as to plead their cause before men; who
speaks comfortably to them, and labours, by
all his words, to strengthen their hands in
God. He assists them to the uttermost of his
power in all things, spiritual and temporal.
He is ready "to spend and be spent for
them;" yea, to lay down his life for their
sake.

6. Thou, O man of God, think on these
things! If thou art already in this way, go on.
If thou hast heretofore mistook the path,
bless God who hath brought thee back! And
now run the race which is set before thee, in
the royal way of universal love. Take heed,
lest thou be either wavering in thy judgement, or straitened in thy bowels: But keep
an even pace, rooted in the faith once de-

Exhortation to cultivate a catholic spirit

livered to the saints, and grounded in love,
in true catholic love, till thou art swallowed
up in love for ever and ever!

JOHN WESLEY,
"LETTER TO A ROMAN CATHOLIC" (1749)

Comment: This published letter was written in the same year (1749) as the sermon on a "Catholic Spirit," and it provides a good illustration of many of the principles that John Wesley laid out in that sermon, applied specifically to relationships between Catholics and Protestants in Ireland, where John Wesley had been preaching and organizing societies.

The sermon on a "Catholic Spirit" asserts that a Christian must be "fixed as the sun in his judgement concerning the main branches of Christian doctrine" (III:1). Elsewhere Wesley could speak of "essential" or "fundamental" doctrines, but the sermon on a "Catholic Spirit" did not give a list of such essential doctrines. A passage from this letter, paragraphs 6 through 10, gives a fair view of the beliefs that he believed were shared in common between Christians. The passage is set as giving the beliefs of "a true Protestant," but at the end of the passage John Wesley asks if these are not the common beliefs of Catholics and Protestants as well. The passage follows, for the most part, the language and structure of the Nicene Creed. It curiously omits reference to the doctrine of original sin (which Wesley would strongly insist on as a necessary Methodist doctrine from the middle of the 1750s), and includes a reference to belief in the perpetual virginity of Mary (common to Catholic doctrine and to many formal Anglican theologies).

Source: Jackson, *Works*, 10:80-86.

1. You have heard ten thousand stories of us who are commonly called Protestants, of which if you believe only one in a thousand, you must think very hardly of us. But this is quite contrary to our Lord's rule, "Judge not, that ye be not judged;" and has many ill consequences; particularly this,—it inclines us to think as hardly of you. Hence we are on both sides less willing to help one another, and more ready to hurt each other. Hence brotherly love is utterly destroyed; and each side, looking on the other as monsters, gives way to anger, hatred, malice, to every unkind affliction; which have frequently broke out in such inhuman barbarities as are scarce named among the Heathens.

2. Now, can nothing be done, even allowing us on both sides to retain our own opinions, for the softening our hearts towards each other, the giving a check to this flood of unkindness, and restoring at least some small degree of love among our neighbours and countrymen? Do not you wish for this? Are you not fully convinced, that malice, hatred, revenge, bitterness, whether in us or in you, in our hearts or yours, are an abomination to the Lord? Be our opinions right, or be they wrong, these tempers are undeniably wrong. They are the broad road that leads to destruction, to the nethermost hell.

3. I do not suppose all the bitterness is on your side. I know there is too much on our

Occasion of the letter: misunderstanding and unkindness between Catholics and Protestants

side also; so much, that I fear many Protestants (so called) will be angry at me too, for writing to you in this manner; and will say, "It is showing you too much favour; you deserve no such treatment at our hands."

Blame for these misunderstandings lies on both sides

4. But I think you do. I think you deserve the tenderest regard I can show, were it only because the same God hath raised you and me from the dust of the earth, and has made us both capable of loving and enjoying him to eternity; were it only because the Son of God has bought you and me with his own blood. How much more, if you are a person fearing God, (as without question many of you are,) and studying to have a conscience voice of offence towards God and towards man?

5. I shall therefore endeavour, as mildly and inoffensively as I can, to remove in some measure the ground of your unkindness, by plainly declaring what our belief and what our practice is; that you may see, we are not altogether such monsters as perhaps you imagined us to be.

A true Protestant may express his belief in these or the like words:—

6. As I am assured that there is an infinite and independent Being, and that it is impossible there should be more than one; so I believe, that this One God is the Father of all things, especially of angels and men; that he is in a peculiar manner the Father of those whom he regenerates by his Spirit,

Faith in God the Father

whom he adopts in his Son, as co-heirs with him, and crowns with an eternal inheritance; but in a still higher sense the Father of his only Son, whom he hath begotten from eternity.

I believe this Father of all, not only to be able to do whatsoever pleased him, but also to have an eternal right of making what and when and how he pleased, and of possessing and disposing of all that he has made; and that he of his own goodness created heaven and earth, and all that is therein.

7. I believe that Jesus of Nazareth was the Saviour of the world, the Messiah so long foretold; that, being anointed with the Holy Ghost, he was a Prophet, revealing to us the whole will of God; that he was a Priest, who gave himself a sacrifice for sin, and still makes intercession for transgressors; that he is a King, who has all power in heaven and in earth, and will reign till he has subdued all things to himself.

Faith in Jesus Christ

I believe he is the proper, natural Son of God, God of God, very God of very God; and that he is the Lord of all, having absolute, supreme, universal dominion over all things; but more peculiarly our Lord, who believe in him, both by conquest, purchase, and voluntary obligation.

Affirmation of the complete divinity of Jesus Christ (following the Nicene Creed)

I believe that he was made man, joining the human nature with the divine in one person; being conceived by the singular operation of the Holy Ghost, and born of the blessed Virgin Mary, who, as well after as before she brought him forth, continued a pure and unspotted virgin.

I believe he suffered inexpressible pains both of body and soul, and at last death, even the death of the cross, at the time that Pontius Pilate governed Judea, under the Roman Emperor; that his body was then laid in the grave, and his soul went to the place of separate spirits; that the third day he rose again from the dead; that he ascended into heaven; where he remains in the midst of the throne of God, in the highest power and glory, as Mediator till the end of the world, as God to all eternity; that, in the end, he will come down from heaven, to judge every man according to his works; both those who shall be then alive, and all who have died before that day.

Affirmation of the integrity of divine and human natures in the unity of the one Person of Jesus Christ (following the "Definition of Faith" of the Council Chalcedon, AD 451)

8. I believe the infinite and eternal Spirit of God, equal with the Father and the Son, to be not only perfectly holy in himself, but the immediate cause of all holiness in us; enlightening our understandings, rectifying our wills and affections, renewing our natures, uniting our persons to Christ, assuring us of the adoption of sons, leading us in our actions; purifying and sanctifying our souls and bodies, to a full and eternal enjoyment of God.

Faith in the Holy Spirit

9. I believe that Christ by his Apostles gathered unto himself a Church, to which he has continually added such as shall be saved; that this catholic, that is, universal,

Affirmation of the Church

Church, extending to all nations and all ages, is holy in all its members, who have fellowship with God the Father, Son, and Holy Ghost; that they have fellowship with the holy angels, who constantly minister to these heirs of salvation; and with all the living members of Christ on earth, as well as all who are departed in his faith and fear.

10. I believe God forgives all the sins of them that truly repent and unfeignedly believe his holy gospel; and that, at the last day, all men shall rise again, every one with his own body.

Affirmation of God's forgiveness for those who truly believe the Gospel

I believe, that as the unjust shall, after their resurrection, be tormented in hell for ever, so the just shall enjoy inconceivable happiness in the presence of God to all eternity.

Affirmation of the eternal state of happiness for the just and eternal condemnation for the unjust

11. Now, is there any thing wrong in this? Is there any one point which you do not believe as well as we?

But you think we ought to believe more. We will not now enter into the dispute. Only let me ask, If a man sincerely believes thus much, and practises accordingly, can any one possibly persuade you to think that such a man shall perish everlastingly?

12. "But does he practice accordingly?" If he does not, we grant all his faith will not save him. And this leads me to show you, in few and plain words, what the practice of a true Protestant is.

I say, a *true Protestant*; for I disclaim all
common swearers, Sabbath-breakers,
drunkards; all whoremongers, liars, cheats,
extortioners; in a word, all that live in open
sin. These are no Protestants; they are no
Christians at all. Give them their own name;
they are open Heathens. They are the curse
of the nation, the bane of society, the shame
of mankind, the scum of the earth.

13. A true Protestant believes in God, has a
full confidence in his mercy, fears him with
a filial fear, and loves him with all his soul.
He worships God in spirit and in truth, in
everything gives him thanks; calls upon him
with his heart as well as his lips, at all times
and in all places; honours his holy name
and his word, and serves him truly all the
days of his life.

Moral character of a
"true Protestant" (a true
Christian)

Now, do not you yourself approve of this? Is
there any one point you can condemn? Do
not you practice as well as approve of it?
Can you ever be happy if you do not? Can
you ever expect true peace in this, or glory
in the world to come, if you do not believe in
God through Christ? if you do not thus fear
and love God? My dear friend, consider, I
am not persuading you to leave or change
your religion, but to follow after that fear
and love of God without which all religion is
vain. I say not a word to you about your
opinions or outward manner of worship.
But I say, all worship is an abomination to
the Lord, unless you worship him in spirit
and in truth; with your heart, as well as your

lips; with your spirit, and with your understanding also. Be your form of worship what it will, but in everything give him thanks; else it is all but lost labour. Use whatever outward observances you please, but put your whole trust in him; but honour his holy name and his word, and serve him truly all the days of your life.

14. Again: A true Protestant loves his neighbour, that is, every man, friend or enemy, good or bad, as himself, as he loves his own soul, as Christ loved us. And as Christ laid down his life for us, so is he ready to lay down his life for his brethren. He shows this love, by doing to all men, in all points, as he would they should do unto him. He loves, honours, and obeys his father and mother, and helps them to the uttermost of his power. He honours and obeys the King, and all that are put in authority under him. He cheerfully submits to all his Governors, Teachers, spiritual Pastors, and Masters. He behaves lowly and reverently to all his betters. He hurts nobody, by word or deed. He is true and just in all his dealings. He bears no malice or hatred in his heart. He abstains from all evil speaking, lying and slandering; neither is guile found in his mouth. Knowing his body to be the temple of the Holy Ghost, he keeps it in sobriety, temperance, and chastity. He does not desire other men's goods; but is content with that he hath; labours to get his own living, and to do the whole will of God in that state of life unto which it has pleased God to call him.

15. Have you any thing to reprove in this? Are you not herein even as he? If not, (tell the truth,) are you not condemned both by God and your own conscience? Can you fall short of anyone point hereof without falling short of being a Christian?

Come, my brother, and let us reason together. Are you right if you only love your friend and hate your enemy? Do not even the Heathens and publicans so? You are called to love your enemies; to bless them that curse you, and to pray for them that despitefully use you and persecute you. But are you not disobedient to the heavenly calling? Does your tender love to all men, not only the good, but also the evil and unthankful, approve you the child of your Father which is in heaven? Otherwise, whatever you believe and whatever you practise, you are of your father the devil. Are you ready to lay down your life for your brethren? And do you do unto all as you would they should do unto you? If not, do not deceive your own soul: You are but a Heathen still. Do you love, honour, and obey your father and mother, and help them to the utmost of your power? Do you honour and obey all in authority? all your Governors, spiritual Pastors, and Masters? Do you behave lowly and reverently to all your betters? Do you hurt nobody, by word or deed? Are you true and just in all your dealings? Do you take care to pay whatever you owe? Do you feel no malice, or envy, or revenge, no hatred or bitterness to any man? If you do, it is plain you are not of

God: For all these are the tempers of the devil. Do you speak the truth from your heart to all men, and that in tenderness and love? Are you "an Israelite indeed, in whom is no guile?" Do you keep your body in sobriety, temperance, and chastity, as knowing it is the temple of the Holy Ghost, and that, if any man defile the temple of God, him will God destroy? Have you learned, in every state wherein you are, therewith to be content? Do you labour to get your own living, abhorring idleness as you abhor hell-fire? The devil tempts other men; but an idle man tempts the devil. An idle man's brain is the devil's shop, where he is continually working mischief. Are you not slothful in business? Whatever your hand finds to do, do you do it with your might? And do you do all as unto the Lord, as a sacrifice unto God, acceptable in Christ Jesus?

This, and this alone, is the old religion. This is true, primitive Christianity. O when shall it spread over all the earth! When shall it be found both in us and you? Without waiting for others, let each of us, by the grace of God, amend one.

16. Are we not thus far agreed? Let us thank God for this, and receive it as a fresh token of His love. But if God still loveth us, we ought also to love one another. We ought, without this endless jangling about opinions, to provoke one another to love and to good works. Let the points wherein we dif-

fer stand aside; here are enough wherein we agree, enough to be the ground of every Christian temper, and of every Christian action.

O brethren, let us not still fall out by the way! I hope to see you in heaven. And if I practice the religion above described, you dare not say I shall go to hell. You cannot think so. None can persuade you to it. Your own conscience tells you the contrary. Then if we cannot as yet think alike in all things, at least we may love alike. Herein we cannot possibly do amiss. For of one point none can doubt a moment,—"God is love; and he that dwelleth in love, dwelleth in God, and God in him."

17. In the name, then, and in the strength of God, let us resolve, First, not to hurt one another; to do nothing unkind or unfriendly to each other, nothing which we would not have done to ourselves: Rather let us endeavour after every instance of a kind, friendly, and Christian behaviour towards each other.

Specific resolutions that may help relationships between Catholics and Protestants

Let us resolve, Secondly, God being our helper, to speak nothing harsh or unkind of each other. The sure way to avoid this, is to say all the good we can, both of and to one another: In all our conversation, either with or concerning each other, to use only the language of love; to speak with all softness and tenderness; with the most endearing expression which is consistent with truth and sincerity.

Let us, Thirdly, resolve to harbour no unkind thought, no unfriendly temper, towards each other. Let us lay the axe to the root of the tree; let us examine all that rises in our heart, and suffer no disposition there which is contrary to tender affection. Then shall we easily refrain from unkind actions and words, when the very root of bitterness is cut up.

Let us, Fourthly, endeavour to help each other on in whatever we are agreed leads to the kingdom. So far as we can, let us always rejoice to strengthen each other's hands in God. Above all, let us each take heed to himself, (since each must give an account of himself to God,) that he fall not short of the religion of love; that he be not condemned in that he himself approveth. O let you and I (whatever others do) press on to the prize of our high calling! that, being justified by faith, we may have peace with God through our Lord Jesus Christ; that we may rejoice in God through Jesus Christ, by whom we have received the atonement; that the love of God may be shed abroad in our hearts by the Holy Ghost which is given unto us. Let us count all things but loss for the excellency of the knowledge of Jesus Christ our Lord; being ready for him to suffer the loss of all things, and counting them but dung, that we may win Christ.

I am

Your affectionate servant, for
Christ's sake.

Dublin, *July* 18, 1749.

JOHN WESLEY, SERMON ON "THE SCRIPTURE WAY OF SALVATION" (1765)

Comment: The passage given above from the "Letter to a Roman Catholic" gives an account of the beliefs John Wesley believed were widely shared between Christians. The following sermon, by contrast, offers what is widely agreed to be the best overall description of John Wesley's understanding of the "way of salvation," the Wesleys' most distinctive contribution to Christian spirituality. Section I, answering the question, "What is Salvation?" describes the way of salvation in three stages or phases under the headings of 1) "preventing" grace (Methodists would later say "prevenient" grace), that is, God's grace coming before justification and preparing a person for salvation, 2) justifying grace, that is, God's grace offering pardon for past sins, and 3) sanctifying grace, that is, God's grace that leads the Christian to greater and greater holiness. This understanding of the way of salvation lies at the heart of historic Wesleyan spirituality, often appearing, for example, in an organizational scheme for Methodist hymnals under the general heading of "The Christian Life."

This sermon may be compared to an earlier sermon on the same scripture text entitled "Salvation by Faith" (1738), which is traditionally given as the first sermon in collected editions of John Wesley's works. The 1738 sermon has in fact the same two first sections as this sermon, that is, "What is Faith?" and "What is salvation?" (though in reverse order from this sermon). But the language and careful distinctions made in the sermon given here reflect John Wesley's much more refined thought and use of terms.

Source: Jackson, *Works*, 6:43-54.

"Ye are saved through faith."—Ephesians ii. 8.

1. NOTHING can be more intricate, complex, and hard to be understood, than religion, as it has been often described. And this is not only true concerning the religion of the Heathens, even many of the wisest of them, but concerning the religion of those also who were, in some sense, Christians; yea, and men of great name in the Christian world; men who seemed to be pillars thereof. Yet how easy to be understood, how plain and simple a thing, is the genuine religion of Jesus Christ; provided only that we take it in its native form, just as it is described in the oracles of God! It is exactly suited, by the wise Creator and Governor of the world, to the weak understanding and narrow capacity of man in his present state. How observable is this, both with regard to the end it proposes, and the means to attain that end! The end is, in one word, salvation; the means to attain it, faith.

2. It is easily discerned, that these two little words, I mean faith and salvation, include the substance of all the Bible, the marrow, as it were, of the whole Scripture. So much the more should we take all possible care to avoid all mistake concerning them, and to

Introduction

form a true and accurate judgement concerning both the one and the other.

3. Let us then seriously inquire,

I. What is salvation?
II. What is that faith whereby we are saved? And,
III. How are we saved by it?

I. 1. And, first, let us inquire, What is salvation? The salvation which is here spoken of is not what is frequently understood by that word, the going to heaven, eternal happiness. It is not the soul's going to paradise, termed by our Lord, "Abraham's bosom." It is not a blessing which lies on the other side death; or, as we usually speak, in the other world. The very words of the text itself put this beyond all question: "Ye *are saved*." It is not something at a distance: It is a present thing; a blessing which, through the free mercy of God, ye are now in possession of. Nay, the words may be rendered, and that with equal propriety, "Ye *have been* saved": So that the salvation which is here spoken of might be extended to the entire work of God, from the first dawning of grace in the soul, till it is consummated in glory.

I. What is salvation?

2. If we take this in its utmost extent, it will include all that is wrought in the soul by what is frequently termed "natural conscience," but more properly, "preventing grace";—all the drawings of the Father; the desires after God, which, if we yield to them, increase more and more;—all that light wherewith the Son of God "enlighteneth

"Preventing" (or "prevenient") grace: grace coming before our justification

every one that cometh into the world;"
showing every man "to do justly, to love
mercy, and to walk humbly with his God";—
all the convictions which His Spirit, from
time to time, works in every child of man;
although it is true, the generality of men
stifle them as soon as possible, and after a
while forget, or at least deny, that they ever
had them at all.

3. But we are at present concerned only with
that salvation which the Apostle is directly
speaking of. And this consists of two general
parts, justification and sanctification.

Justification is another word for pardon. It
is the forgiveness of all our sins; and, what
is necessarily implied therein, our acceptance with God. The price whereby this hath
been procured for us (commonly termed the
meritorious cause of our justification,) is
the blood and righteousness of Christ; or, to
express it a little more clearly, all that Christ
hath done and suffered for us, till he
"poured out His soul for the transgressors."
The immediate effects of justification are,
the peace of God, a "peace that passeth all
understanding," and a "rejoicing in hope of
the glory of God" "with joy unspeakable and
full of glory."

Justification

4. And at the same time that we are justified, yea, in that very moment, sanctification begins. In that instant we are born
again, born from above, born of the Spirit:
there is a *real* as well as a *relative* change.
We are inwardly renewed by the power of

Sanctification

God. We feel "the love of God shed abroad in our heart by the Holy Ghost which is given unto us"; producing love to all mankind, and more especially to the children of God; expelling the love of the world, the love of pleasure, of ease, of honour, of money, together with pride, anger, self-will, and every other evil temper; in a word, changing the earthly, sensual, devilish mind, into "the mind which was in Christ Jesus."

5. How naturally do those who experience such a change imagine that all sin is gone; that it is utterly rooted out of their heart, and has no more any place therein! How easily do they draw that inference, "I *feel* no sin; therefore, I *have* none: it does not *stir*; therefore it does not *exist*: it has no *motion*; therefore, it has no *being*!"

6. But it is seldom long before they are undeceived, finding sin was only suspended, not destroyed. Temptations return, and sin revives; showing it was but stunned before, not dead. They now feel two principles in themselves, plainly contrary to each other; "the flesh lusting against the Spirit"; nature opposing the grace of God. They cannot deny, that although they still feel power to believe in Christ, and to love God; and although His "Spirit" still "witnesses with their spirits, that they are children of God"; yet they feel in themselves sometimes pride or self-will, sometimes anger or unbelief. They find one or more of these frequently *stirring* in their heart, though not *conquer-*

ing; yea, perhaps, "thrusting sore at them that they may fall"; but the Lord is their help.

7. How exactly did Macarius, fourteen hundred years ago, describe the present experience of the children of God! "The unskilful," or unexperienced, "when grace operates, presently imagine they have no more sin. Whereas they that have discretion cannot deny, that even we who have the grace of God may be molested again.—For we have often had instances of some among the brethren, who have experienced such grace as to affirm that they had no sin in them; and yet, after all, when they thought themselves entirely freed from it, the corruption that lurked within was stirred up anew, and they were well-nigh burned up."

8. From the time of our being born again, the gradual work of sanctification takes place. We are enabled "by the Spirit" to "mortify the deeds of the body," of our evil nature; and as we are more and more dead to sin, we are more and more alive to God. We so on from grace to grace, while we are careful to "abstain from all appearance of evil," and are "zealous of good works," as we have opportunity, doing good to all men; while we walk in all His ordinances blameless, therein worshipping Him in spirit and in truth; while we take up our cross, and deny ourselves every pleasure that does not lead us to God.

9. It is thus that we wait for entire sanctification; for a full salvation from all our sins,—
from pride, self-will, anger, unbelief; or, as
the Apostle expresses it, "go unto perfection." But what is perfection? The word has
various senses: Here it means perfect love.
It is love excluding sin; love filling the heart,
taking up the whole capacity of the soul. It
is love "rejoicing evermore, praying without
ceasing, in every thing giving thanks."

Entire sanctification

II. But what is faith through which we are
saved? This is the Second point to be considered.

II. What is faith?

1. Faith, in general, is defined by the
Apostle, πραγμάτων ἔλεγχος οὐ
βλεπωμένων. *An evidence*, a divine *evidence and conviction* (the word means both)
of things not seen; not visible, not perceiv-
able either by sight, or by any other of the
external senses. It implies both a supernatural *evidence* of God, and of the things of
God; a kind of spiritual *light* exhibited to
the soul, and a supernatural *sight* or per-
ception thereof. Accordingly, the Scripture
speaks of God's giving sometimes light,
sometimes a power of discerning it. So St.
Paul: "God, who commanded light to shine
out of darkness, hath shined in our hearts,
to give us the light of the knowledge of the
glory of God in the face of Jesus Christ."
And elsewhere the same Apostle speaks of
"the eyes of" our "understanding being
opened." By this two-fold operation of the
Holy Spirit, having the eyes of our soul both

Faith in a general sense
is a kind of spiritual
sense or sight

opened and *enlightened*, we see the things which the natural "eye hath not seen, neither the ear heard." We have a prospect of the invisible things of God; we see the *spiritual world*, which is all round about us, and yet no more discerned by our natural faculties than if it had no being. And we see the *eternal world*; piercing through the veil which hangs between time and eternity. Clouds and darkness then rest upon it no more, but we already see the glory which shall be revealed.

2. Taking the word in a more particular sense, faith is a divine *evidence* and *conviction* not only that "God was in Christ, reconciling the world unto Himself," but also that Christ loved me, and gave Himself for me. It is by this faith (whether we term it the *essence*, or rather a *property* thereof) that we *receive Christ*; that we receive Him in all His offices, as our Prophet, Priest, and King. It is by this that He is "made of God unto us wisdom, and righteousness, and sanctification, and redemption."

Faith in a specifically Christian sense has Christ as its object

3. "But is this the *faith of assurance*, or *faith of adherence*?" The Scripture mentions no such distinction. The Apostle says, "There is one faith, and one hope of our calling"; one Christian, saving faith; "as there is one Lord," in whom we believe, and "one God and Father of us all." And it is certain, this faith necessarily implies an *assurance* (which is here only another word for *evidence*, it being hard to tell the difference

between them) that Christ loved me, and gave himself for me. For "he that believeth" with the true living faith "hath the witness in himself": "The Spirit witnesseth with his spirit that he is a child of God." "Because he is a son, God hath sent forth the Spirit of His Son into his heart, crying, Abba, Father;" giving him an assurance that he is so, and a childlike confidence in him. But let it be observed, that, in the very nature of the thing, the assurance goes before the confidence. For a man cannot have a childlike confidence in God till he knows he is a child of God. Therefore, confidence, trust, reliance, adherence, or whatever else it be called, is not the first, as some have supposed, but the second, branch or act of faith.

4. It is by this faith we are saved, justified, and sanctified; taking that word in its highest sense. But how are we justified and sanctified by faith? This is our third head of inquiry. And this being the main point in question, and a point of no ordinary importance, it will not be improper to give it a more distinct and particular consideration.

III. 1. And, First, how are we justified by faith? In what sense is this to be understood? I answer, Faith is the condition, and the only condition, of justification. It is the *condition*: None is justified but he that believes: without faith no man is justified. And it is the *only condition*: This alone is sufficient for justification. Every one that believes is justified, whatever else he has or

III. Answers to specific questions

has not. In other words: No man is justified till he believes; every man when he believes is justified.

2. "But does not God command us to repent also? Yea, and to 'bring forth fruits meet for repentance'—to cease, for instance, from doing evil, and learn to do well? And is not both the one and the other of the utmost necessity, insomuch that if we willingly neglect either, we cannot reasonably expect to be justified at all? But if this be so, how can it be said that faith is the only condition of justification?"

God does undoubtedly command us both to repent, and to bring forth fruits meet for repentance; which if we willingly neglect, we cannot reasonably expect to be justified at all: Therefore both repentance, and fruits meet for repentance, are, in some sense, necessary to justification. But they are not necessary in the *same sense* with faith, nor in the *same degree*. Not in the same degree; for those fruits are only necessary *conditionally*; if there be time and opportunity for them. Otherwise a man may be justified without them, as was the *thief* upon the cross (if we may call him so; for a late writer has discovered that he was no thief, but a very honest and respectable person!); but he cannot be justified without faith; this is impossible. Likewise, let a man have ever so much repentance, or ever so many of the fruits meet for repentance, yet all this does not at all avail; he is not justified till he be-

lieves. But the moment he believes, with or
without those fruits, yea, with more or less
repentance, he is justified.–Not in the *same
sense*; for repentance and its fruits are only
remotely necessary; necessary in order to
faith; whereas faith is *immediately* and *directly* necessary to justification. It remains,
that faith is the only condition, which is *immediately* and *proximately* necessary to
justification.

3. "But do you believe we are sanctified by
faith? We know you believe that we are justified by faith; but do not you believe, and
accordingly teach, that we are sanctified by
our works?" So it has been roundly and
vehemently affirmed for these five-and-
twenty years: But I have constantly declared
just the contrary; and that in all manner of
ways. I have continually testified in private
and in public, that we are sanctified as well
as justified by faith. And indeed the one of
those great truths does exceedingly illustrate the other. Exactly as we are justified by
faith, so are we sanctified by faith. Faith is
the condition, and the only condition, of
sanctification, exactly as it is of justification.
It is the *condition*: none is sanctified but he
that believes; with out faith no man is sanctified. And it is the *only condition*: This
alone is sufficient for sanctification. Every
one that believes is sanctified, whatever else
he has or has not. In other words, no man is
sanctified till he believes: every man when
he believes is sanctified.

4. "But is there not a repentance consequent upon, as well as a repentance previous to, justification? And is it not incumbent on all that are justified to be 'zealous of good works'? Yea, are not these so necessary, that if a man willingly neglect them he cannot reasonably expect that he shall ever be sanctified in the full sense; that is, perfected in love? Nay, can he grow at all in grace, in the loving knowledge of our Lord Jesus Christ? Yea, can he retain the grace which God has already given him? Can he continue in the faith which he has received, or in the favour of God. Do not you yourself allow all this, and continually assert it? But, if this be so, how can it be said that faith is the only condition of sanctification?"

5. I do allow all this, and continually maintain it as the truth of God. I allow there is a repentance consequent upon, as well as a repentance previous to, justification. It is incumbent on all that are justified to be zealous of good works. And there are so necessary, that if a man willingly neglect them, he cannot reasonably expect that he shall ever be sanctified; he cannot grow in grace, in the image of God, the mind which was in Christ Jesus; nay, he cannot retain the grace he has received; he cannot continue in faith, or in the favour of God.

What is the inference we must draw herefrom? Why, that both repentance, rightly understood, and the practice of all good works,—works of piety, as well as works of mercy (now properly so called, since they spring from faith), are, in some sense, necessary to sanctification.

6. I say, "repentance rightly understood"; for this must not be confounded with the former repentance. The repentance consequent upon justification is widely different from that which is antecedent to it. This implies no guilt, no sense of condemnation, no consciousness of the wrath of God. It does not suppose any doubt of the favour of God, or any "fear that hath torment." It is properly a conviction, wrought by the Holy Ghost, of the *sin* which still *remains* in our heart; of the φρωνῆμα σαρκός, *the carnal mind*, which "does still *remain*" (as our Church speaks) "even in them that are regenerate"; although it does no longer *reign*; it has not now dominion over them. It is a conviction of our proneness to evil, of an heart bent to backsliding, of the still continuing tendency of the flesh to lust against the spirit. Sometimes, unless we continually watch and pray, it lusteth to pride, sometimes to anger, sometimes to love of the world, love of ease, love of honour, or love of pleasure more than of God. It is a conviction of the tendency of our heart to self-will, to Atheism, or idolatry; and above all, to unbelief, whereby, in a thousand ways, and under a thousand pretenses, we are ever departing, more or less, from the living God.

7. With this conviction of the sin remaining in our hearts, there is joined a clear convic-

tion of the sin remaining in our lives; still *cleaving* to all our words and actions. In the best of these we now discern a mixture of evil, either in the spirit, the matter, or the manner of them; something that could not endure the righteous judgement of God, were He extreme to mark what is done amiss. Where we least suspected it, we find a taint of pride or self-will, of unbelief or idolatry; so that we are now more ashamed of our best duties than formerly of our worst sins: and hence we cannot but feel that these are so far from having anything meritorious in them, yea, so far from being able to stand in sight of the divine justice, that for those also we should be guilty before God, were it not for the blood of the covenant.

8. Experience shows that, together with this conviction of sin *remaining* in our hearts, and *cleaving* to all our words and actions; as well as the guilt which on account thereof we should incur, were we not continually sprinkled with the atoning blood; one thing more is implied in this repentance; namely, a conviction of our helplessness, of our utter inability to think one good thought, or to form one good desire; and much more to speak one word aright, or to perform one good action, but through his free, almighty grace, first preventing us, and then accompanying us every moment.

9. "But what good works are those, the practice of which you affirm to be necessary to

sanctification?" First, all works of piety;
such as public prayer, family prayer, and
praying in our closet; receiving the supper
of the Lord; searching the Scriptures, by
hearing, reading, meditating; and using
such a measure of fasting or abstinence as
our bodily health allows.

10. Secondly, all works of mercy; whether
they relate to the bodies or souls of men;
such as feeding the hungry, clothing the naked, entertaining the stranger, visiting those
that are in prison, or sick, or variously af-
flicted; such as the endeavouring to instruct
the ignorant, to awaken the stupid sinner, to
quicken the lukewarm, to confirm the
wavering, to comfort the feeble-minded, to
succour the tempted, or contribute in any
manner to the saving of souls from death.
This is the repentance, and these the "fruits
meet for repentance," which are necessary
to full sanctification. This is the way
wherein God hath appointed His children to
wait for complete salvation.

11. Hence may appear the extreme mis-
chievousness of that seemingly innocent
opinion, that there is no sin in a believer;
that all sin is destroyed, root and branch,
the moment a man is justified. By totally
preventing that repentance, it quite blocks
up the way to sanctification. There is no
place for repentance in him who believes
there is no sin either in his life or heart:
Consequently, there is no place for his being

perfected in love, to which that repentance is indispensably necessary.

12. Hence it may likewise appear, that there is no possible danger in *thus* expecting full salvation. For suppose we were mistaken, suppose no such blessing ever was or can be attained, yet we lose nothing: Nay, that very expectation quickens us in using all the talents which God has given us; yea, in improving them all; so that when our Lord cometh, He will receive his own with increase.

13. But to return. Though it be allowed, that both this repentance and its fruits are necessary to full salvation; yet they are not necessary either in the same sense with faith, or in the same degree:—Not in the same degree; for these fruits are only necessary conditionally, if there be time and opportunity for them; otherwise a man may be sanctified without them. But he cannot be sanctified without faith. Likewise, let a man have ever so much of this repentance, or ever so many good works, yet all this does not at all avail: he is not sanctified till he believes. But the moment he believes, with or without those fruits, yea, with more or less of this repentance, he is sanctified.—Not in the same sense; for this repentance and these fruits are only remotely necessary,—necessary in order to the continuance of his faith, as well as the increase of it; whereas faith is immediately and directly necessary to sanctification. It remains, that faith is the only condi-

tion which is immediately and proximately necessary to sanctification.

14. "But what is that faith whereby we are sanctified,—saved from sin, and perfected in love?" It is a divine evidence and conviction, First, that God hath promised it in the Holy Scripture. Till we are thoroughly satisfied of this, there in no moving one step further. And one would imagine there needed not one word more to satisfy a reasonable man of this, than the ancient promise, "Then will I circumcise thy heart, and the heart of thy seed, to love the Lord thy God with all thy heart, and with all thy soul, and with all thy mind." How clearly does this express the being perfected in love!—how strongly imply the being saved from all sin! For as long as love takes up the whole heart, what room is there for sin therein?

15. It is a divine evidence and conviction, Secondly, that what God hath promised he is able to perform. Admitting, therefore, that "with men it is impossible" to "bring a clean thing out of an unclean," to purify the heart from all sin, and to fill it with all holiness; yet this creates no difficulty in the case, seeing "with God all things are possible." And surely no one ever imagined it was possible to any power less than that of the Almighty! But if God speaks, it shall be done. God saith, "Let there be light; and there" is "light"!

16. It is, Thirdly, a divine evidence and conviction that He is able and willing to do it

now. And why not? Is not a moment to him
the same as a thousand years? He cannot
want more time to accomplish whatever is
His will. And He cannot want or stay for any
more worthiness or fitness in the persons he
is pleased to honour. We may therefore
boldly say, at any point of time, "Now is the
day of salvation!" "To-day, if ye will hear his
voice, harden not your hearts!" "Behold, all
things are now ready; come unto the mar-
riage!"

17. To this confidence, that God is both able
and willing to sanctify us now, there needs
to be added one thing more,—a divine evidence and conviction that he doeth it. In that
hour it is done: God says to the inmost soul,
"According to thy faith be it unto thee!"
Then the soul is pure from every spot of sin;
it is clean "from all unrighteousness." The
believer then experiences the deep meaning
of those solemn words, "If we walk in the
light as He is in the light, we have fellowship
one with another, and the blood of Jesus
Christ His Son cleanseth us from all sin."

18. "But does God work this great work in
the soul gradually or instantaneously?" Perhaps it may be gradually wrought in some; I
mean in this sense,—they do not advert to
the particular moment wherein sin ceases to
be. But it us infinitely desirable, were it the
will of God, that it should be done instantaneously; that the Lord should destroy sin
"by the breath of his mouth," in a moment,
in the twinkling of an eye. And so he gener-

ally does; a plain fact, of which there is evidence enough to satisfy any unprejudiced
person. Thou therefore look for it every moment! Look for it in the way above described; in all those good works whereunto
thou art "created anew in Christ Jesus."
There is then no danger: you can be no
worse, if you are no better, for that expectation. For were you to be disappointed of
your hope, still you lose nothing. But you
shall not be disappointed of your hope: It
will come, and will not tarry. Look for it
then every day, every hour, every moment!
Why not this hour, this moment? Certainly
you may look for it now, if you believe it is
by faith. And by this token you may surely
know whether you seek it by faith or by
works. If by works, you want something to
be done first, before you are sanctified. You
think, I must first be or do thus or thus.
Then you are seeking it by works unto this
day. If you seek it by faith, you may expect it
as you are; and expect it now. It is of importance to observe, that there is an inseparable connexion between these three
points,—expect it by faith; expect it as you
are; and expect it now! To deny one of them,
is to deny them all; to allow one, is to allow
them all. Do you believe we are sanctified by
faith? Be true then to your principle; and
look for this blessing just as you are, neither
better nor worse; as a poor sinner that has
still nothing to pay, nothing to plead, but
"Christ *died.*" And if you look for it as you
are, then expect it *now.* Stay for nothing:

Why should you? Christ is ready; and He is
all you want. He is waiting for you: He is at
the door! Let your inmost soul cry out,

Come in, come in, thou heavenly Guest!
    Nor hence again remove;
But sup with me, and let the feast
    Be everlasting love.

JOHN WESLEY, LETTER "TO DR. COKE, MR. ASBURY, AND OUR BRETHREN IN NORTH AMERICA" (1784)

Comment: Although John Wesley had consistently forbidden his preachers to separate from the Church of England, the Methodist movement under his leadership had grown farther and farther from the national Church. This was the source of a very serious and on-going rift between himself and his brother Charles, who had tried to hold Methodism strictly within the bounds of the Church of England.

Almost all Anglican priests, having taken oaths of allegiance to the British crown as a condition of their ordination, left America at the beginning of the Revolutionary War and could not return. American Anglicans of all sorts (including American Methodists) had to find ways to secure ordained clergy in the early 1780s, leading to the foundation of the Protestant Episcopal Church (today's Episcopal Church in the USA) and the Methodist Episcopal Church, from which American Methodist churches are derived.

John Wesley tried, as he explains in the following letter, to secure ordained clergy through the normal processes of the Church of England, but he was not satisfied that these processes would work within a time frame that would resolve the immediate needs of the American Methodists. Having his own theological justification, he proceeded in early September of 1784 to ordain clergy for North America, sending the following letter justifying his actions. Since he was not himself a bishop, his ordinations violated the canons of his own Church, and Charles Wesley could not accept the validity of John's actions.

Source: Jackson, ed., *Works*, 13:251-252.

Bristol, September 10, 1784.

1. By a very uncommon train of providences, many of the provinces of North America are totally disjoined from their mother-country, and erected into independent States. The English Government has no authority over them, either civil or ecclesiastical, any more than over the States of Holland. A civil authority is exercised over them, partly by the Congress, partly by the provincial Assemblies. But no one either exercises or claims any ecclesiastical authority at all. In this peculiar situation some thousands of the inhabitants of these States desire my advice; and in compliance with their desire, I have drawn up a little sketch.

> The independence of the American "provinces" (he will not say the "United States")

2. Lord King's "Account of the Primitive Church" convinced me many years ago, that Bishops and Presbyters are the same order, and consequently have the same right to ordain. For many years I have been importuned, from time to time, to exercise this right, by ordaining part of our Travelling Preachers. But I have still refused, not only for peace' sake, but because I was determined as little as possible to violate the established order of the national Church to which I belonged.

> A theological justification for ordination apart from bishops

3. But the case is widely different between England and North America. Here there are Bishops who have a legal jurisdiction: In America there are none, neither any parish Ministers. So that for some hundred miles together, there is none, either to baptise, or to administer the Lord's supper. Here, therefore, my scruples are at an end; and I conceive myself at full liberty, as I violate no order, and invade no man's right, by appointing and sending labourers into the harvest.

A practical justification: the need for clergy to celebrate the sacraments in North America

4. I have accordingly appointed Dr. Coke and Mr. Francis Asbury to be joint Superintendents over our brethren in North America; as also Richard Whatcoat and Thomas Vasey to act as Elders among them, by baptising and administering the Lord's supper. And I have prepared a Liturgy, little differing from that of the Church of England, (I think, the best constituted national Church in the world,) which I advise all the Travelling Preachers to use on the Lord's day, in all the congregations, reading the Litany only on Wednesdays and Fridays, and praying extempore on all other days. I also advise the Elders to administer the supper of the Lord on every Lord's day.

John Wesley's actions in ordaining clergy and in preparing a liturgy based on the Book of Common Prayer

5. If any one will point out a more rational and scriptural way of feeding and guiding those poor sheep in the wilderness, I will gladly embrace it. At present, I cannot see any better method than that I have taken.

6. It has, indeed, been proposed to desire the English Bishops to ordain part of our Preachers for America. But to this I object, (1.) I desired the Bishop of London to ordain only one; but could not prevail. (2.) If they consented, we know the slowness of their proceedings; but the matter admits of no delay. (3.) If they would ordain them now, they would likewise expect to govern them. And how grievously would this entangle us! (4.) As our American brethren are now totally disentangled both from the State, and from the English hierarchy, we dare not entangle them again, either with the one or the other. They are now at full liberty, simply to follow the Scriptures and the primitive church. And we judge it best that they should stand fast in that liberty wherewith God has so strangely made them free.

JOHN WESLEY.

Reasons why the Anglican process would not work

Still, he thinks Americans are really weird

JOHN WESLEY,
LETTER TO WILLIAM WILBERFORCE (1791)

Comment: The following letter is believed to be the last letter John Wesley wrote. It was composed six days before his death (which was on 2 March 1791). Earlier printed versions of the letter show it as addressed "To a Friend," but the content and context of the letter show the friend to be William Wilberforce, a Member of Parliament and Evangelical leader in the Church of England whose life work was to oppose the slave trade (which parliament banned in 1807) and the institution of slavery (which Parliament abolished in 1833, a few days before Wilberforce's own death.

Source: Jackson, *Works*, 13:153.

LONDON, February 24, 1791.

DEAR SIR,

UNLESS the divine power has raised you up to be as *Athanasius contra mundum*, I see not how you can go through your glorious enterprise, in opposing that execrable villany, which is the scandal of religion, of England, and of human nature. Unless God has raised you up for this very thing, you will be worn-out by the opposition of men and devils. But, "if God be for you, who can be against you?" Are all of them together stronger than God? O "be not weary in well

> *Athanasius contra mundum*: "Athanasius against the world"

doing!" Go on; in the name of God and in the power of his might, till even American slavery (the vilest that ever saw the sun) shall vanish away before it.

Reading this morning a tract, wrote by a poor African, I was particularly struck by that circumstance,—that a man who has a black skin, being wronged or outraged by a white man, can have no redress; it being a law, in all our colonies, that the oath of a black against a white goes for nothing. What villany is this!

That He who has guided you from your youth up, may continue to strengthen you in this and all things, is the prayer of

Dear Sir,

Your affectionate servant.

CPSIA information can be obtained
at www.ICGtesting.com
Printed in the USA
LVOW04s1153200516

489226LV00016B/145/P